W9-AAT-675

3 9048 10065267 0

JUL 1 6

SECRETS OF A FINANCIAL AID PRO

Master the College Funding Process
and Give Your Child Lifelong Financial Skills
Without Losing Your Cool

JODI OKUN

Seal Beach, California

Ordering Information:

Special discounts are available on quantity purchases by corporations, associations, and others. For details, contact the publisher at the address at orders@15thstreetpress.com.

All media requests should be directed to jodi@jodiokun.com.

My views are my own and don't necessarily reflect the views of any brands or corporations mentioned within this book.

Editor and Project Manager: Marla Markman, www.MarlaMarkman.com

Cover and Interior Design: GKS Creative, www.GKSCreative.com

978-0-9973527-0-2 (Hardcover)

978-0-9973527-2-6 (Softcover)

978-0-9973527-1-9 (eBook)

Printed in the United States

FIRST EDITION

20 19 18 17 16 / 10 9 8 7 6 5 4 3 2 1

Okun, Jodi, author.
    Secrets of a financial aid pro : master the college
funding process and give your child lifelong financial
skills without losing your cool / Jodi Okun. -- First
edition.
    pages cm
    Includes index.
    LCCN 2016903556
    ISBN 978-0-9973527-0-2
    ISBN 978-0-9973527-1-9 (ebook)

    1. Student aid--United States. 2. College costs--
United States.   I. Title.

LB2337.4.O48 2016   378.30973
                     QBI16-600048

To my husband,
"You are the sunshine of my life."

Acknowledgments

First and foremost, to my wonderful family that surrounds me: My superhuman husband, Neil, your love allows me to accomplish so much. Randi, Ryan, and Ashley, you are my whole life, and because of you three, I am a better woman every day. Thank you to my mom, Brenda, and my dad, Sandy, for your unconditional love and support.

Writing a book is much more than I imagined. It is long and grueling and requires the endurance of running a marathon. The completion of this book could not have been possible without tremendous support provided by Kathy Reandeau, Marla Markman, and Gwen Moran.

Thanks most of all to Alexandra Teixeira, hired as associate director, but undoubtedly running the company by now. Alexandra, you save me from going crazy, and you contributed more to this book than most people will ever know. #YouRule!

Because of you Ellen Friedman and one early-morning walk, my journey began. Thank you so much for everything: your friendship, collaboration, good humor for what seems like forever, or at least 20-plus years.

To my highly spirited mentors, you give me knowledge and words of encouragement every day. Anyone who achieves greatness had a mentor. Thank you to Maureen McRae Goldberg, Britt Michalean, Peg Fitzpatrick, Gina Becerril, Robin Thompson, Jean Gaudern, and Nancy Medina.

A special thank you to the creative team who made sure the book and I looked good inside and out: Gordon Gallego, Cameron Radice, Sivan Amilani, Taryn Feldt, Mimi El Zein, and Gwyn Snider. Production of this book has been a long journey, and I couldn't have done it without you.

A number of other individuals allow me to call on them regularly for advice, information, and friendship: Rieva Lesonsky and Brian Moran. And thanks to Rob Weiss, Abbe Kalin, and the whole team at Discover, who knew a phone call would start the partnership that has helped my company grow in innumerable ways.

To Melissa Smith, Laurie Raykoff, and Sharon Greenthal, thank you for always being there for me. I cherish our friendship and all the memories we share.

Last, but certainly not least, I want to thank all my clients: They are the extended part of the CFAA family, and I am so grateful for all your continued business and support.

Table of Contents

Foreword: Maureen McRae Goldberg
Executive Director of Financial Aid
Occidental College (retired)   ix

Introduction: Financial Aid Doesn't Have to Be Scary!   1

PART 1: MAKING THE MOST OF THE SCHOOL DAYS
Chapter 1: Yes, It Starts in Middle School   15
Chapter 2: Planning through the High School Years   27
Chapter 3: How Can Seniors Get It All Done?   43
Chapter 4: Get Your Money-Challenged Child Ready for College   61

PART 2: PAYING THE WAY
Chapter 5: How Does All This Work, Anyway?   75
Chapter 6: Taking the Fear Out of the FAFSA   87
Chapter 7: Understanding Different Types of Aid   103
Chapter 8: Are Student Loans a Savior or a Sinkhole?   121

PART 3: OFF AND AWAY
Chapter 9: Why Can't Freshmen Manage Their Money Better?   141
Chapter 10: Financial Reality 101: A Primer for College Seniors 153
Chapter 11: Paying Back Those Student Loans   167
Chapter 12: Congratulations, You Made It!   177

Glossary   179
End Notes   187
Index   189

Foreword

HIGHER EDUCATION IS BELEAGUERED OF LATE: Costs keep rising, family resources keep decreasing, the government keeps regulating, and the demands from all constituencies keeps growing. Financial aid professionals are committed to students and often speak of the joy they find in their jobs. The dream of attending college is impossible without the financial resources to do so. Financial aid is the key that unlocks doors, and those who are in the profession often can't imagine doing anything else but being a part of making dreams come true. Many could move up or move over and start new careers, but most are dedicated to the ideals of access and equity and the opportunities it provides to change lives.

Jodi Okun is such a person. I first met Jodi in a virtual context. She was a student in a UCLA Extension class I taught for their college counseling online certificate program. Unlike most of the students, Jodi was not employed at a high school or college looking to further their own careers. She enrolled in the program because she was about to become an empty-nester and wanted to try something different in this new phase of her life. Many of the students openly admitted that they disliked the technical parts of higher education and considered my course as a requirement to get through, rather than an area they wanted to explore or a field they wanted to enter, but Jodi stood out from her classmates. In an online environment, it is often difficult to distinguish between students, and Jodi would have probably been just another name if she hadn't done something old-fashioned: She picked up the telephone and called me at my office at Occidental College.

She asked if she could take me out for coffee and talk to me about working in the field of financial aid. I think we spent several hours in our first meeting. This led to her volunteering in my office to learn the field, which led to her being employed as a seasonal analyzer. She was an aid administrator trifecta: 1) She enjoyed helping people; 2) she enjoyed the complexities of federal regulations, need analysis, and verification; and 3) she had a personality that flourished in an educational environment. She has since started her own business mentoring students and advising parents, but also is the brand ambassador for Discover Student Loans. It has been my honor to mentor Jodi over the years, and I (and many others) have been a part of her fan club ever since.

Secrets of a Financial Aid Pro comes at a very important time in higher education. Not only is the federal government making major changes in the way federal financial aid is applied for, but states are pulling back on their decades-long financial commitment to higher education. The cost of attending college has sky-rocketed: Fall 2016 will mark private college tuition surpassing $50,000, with total costs exceeding $70,000. Multiply that by the four to six years it takes to put a child through college, then by the number of children you have, and the total begins to daunt even those who have managed to put money aside. Short of the *über* wealthy, who can afford this? That is where financial aid comes in. Only a small percentage of families pay the full cost of education; in many cases, up to 80 percent of enrolled students receive gift aid (grants or scholarships) and additional self-help (loans and work) to reduce costs, based on their ability to contribute. But accessing these funds can appear as daunting as the costs.

There are thousands of colleges in the US, and from low-cost community colleges to high-priced Ivies, they all offer financial assistance. The basic application form is called the Free Application for Federal Student Aid (FAFSA). Note that the first "F" represents "Free," so you shouldn't pay to complete this form. But the second "F" is federal, which means it's a government form, and the federal government sets the rules. It also means that it is an application for "federal" aid, and while many colleges, universities, and states use the FAFSA as a base for eligibility, completing the FAFSA is only one stop on the financial aid journey. *Secrets of a Financial Aid Pro* is your travel guide.

Unlike books written by financial aid professionals whose only experience has been behind the desk or independent financial aid advisors who have never worked in a college environment, Jodi's background combines these two important perspectives and offers one more. She has been in your shoes. Prior to beginning her career as a financial aid professional, she sent two children through the college admission and financial aid process. Once again, a perfect trifecta.

Every stage of higher education is part of a journey. I can recommend no better tour guide than Jodi.

Maureen McRae Goldberg
Executive Director of Financial Aid (retired)
Occidental College

Introduction

Financial Aid Doesn't Have to Be Scary!

BETWEEN MRS. SMITH'S FURIOUS PEN-TAPPING and the number of times Mr. Smith shifted in the chair next to her, I could tell they were nervous. Their daughter, Jill, soon to be a high school senior, was looking out the window, seemingly oblivious to her parents' anxiety. As I looked across the table at them, I knew their question before they even asked it.

"How will we ever pay for college?"

I've been through this scenario hundreds of times, first as a college financial aid counselor and then as an independent consultant helping families navigate the complex—and, for many, frightening—financial aid landscape. I've been involved in making decisions about financial aid, in helping parents and students figure out tough questions about how to pay for school, and as a concerned parent helping her children prepare for college. Throughout, I have found that, regardless of their income or financial circumstances, most people have that same fundamental question. They worry that they make too much to qualify for aid or too little to afford college at all. Understanding how financial aid works and whether they'll qualify for any is especially worrisome and confusing.

The answers are different for each family's individual situation. It's unfortunate that money can be such a stumbling block for so many families seeking higher education for their children. However, that is the reality of the society in which we live. Media attention focuses on rising tuition costs, and the student loan debt burden seems to capture headlines every day. Some politicians have even made revamping access to education part of their political platforms.

What's missing from all this noise are solid answers to the pressing questions on everyone's mind. How can we afford college for our children? How do we navigate this complicated financial aid system? And how do we make the best decisions for our family when it comes to such an important and expensive life decision?

I know that the college application process can be overwhelming and mysterious for most families. Unless you have older children or know somebody in the financial aid field, it can feel daunting to both get your child into college and then find a way to pay for it. Everyone is afraid that one wrong answer or one false step will derail the entire process and lead to disappointment for your child.

It's my job to demystify the process. It's thrilling to help a family figure out how their child will be able to attend the college of their dreams. I love seeing the looks on their faces in the photos they send me from their college graduation ceremonies. As I think back over the hundreds of financial aid counseling sessions, face-to-face discussions, Free Application for Federal Student Aid (FAFSA) form discussions, and scholarship applications, I feel blessed to have been able to help and thankful I had the knowledge that could calm their concerns and provide a clear course of action. Now, it's time to do that for you.

A PEEK BEHIND THE CURTAIN

Earlier in my professional career, I was one of those people making the decisions about what financial aid went to which students. It was pretty amazing how many people didn't understand the process or how to make it work to their benefit. Many times, they spent time, money, and energy on activities that were not included in the need analysis formula or when making financial aid decisions.

What do you see in your mind when you think of a financial aid office? Perhaps it's the image of an ivy-covered building where dozens of people are sorting through stacks of paper or huddled around conference room tables looking at student files. Well, financial aid offices are often frenetically busy places with small staffs reviewing thousands and thousands of files. When I did the job, I might get all the students whose last names began with M through O, or I might get a random grouping of several hundred student files at a time. We worked with paper files, although today some are electronic, depending on the school.

After receiving my assigned files, I was responsible for analyzing them according to certain criteria. Depending on how the school prioritized income and assets, I would typically be looking at financial data—tax returns, annual income, investments and other assets, number of dependents, and other factors—to determine how much a family could, as calculated, afford to pay for a child's education. In cases of merit aid, which are handled by the admissions team and not the financial aid office, the college would also look at the student's academic record. We used various federal-regulated benchmarks and methodology, the school's internal system, and institutional methodology developed by the College Board to create an award package that might include a combination of grants, scholarships, loans, and work-study programs. We had thresholds, and once the money was committed, that was it. With a few exceptions, we couldn't make more awards. Some schools award aid on a first-come, first-served basis, so families that acted earlier fared better than those who were late to the game.

Families typically received their financial aid packages in March. Then, an onslaught of calls would begin. Parents either wanted to know why they didn't get more money or explain how their circumstances changed because of a job loss or other hardship, necessitating another review of their financials and, possibly, another award. Of course, this varies depending on the state and school. For example, at some colleges in California, you need to commit to the school before they will review a special circumstance request. Commitment dates are usually around May 1.

Continuing students generally don't get their financial aid packages until June or July, then start school in August. In general, freshman year is often a base year, and schools will try to give you the same award if they can. No school wants to lose a good student for any reason, especially financial constraints. However, if your financial situation changed significantly, for better or worse, the award is likely to change. If everything stays relatively the same, your award should stay relatively the same.

GETTING THE MOST OUT OF THIS BOOK

This book is designed to be a reference that's easily accessible, no matter where you are in the college financial aid process. We're tackling this subject in three parts:

1. The first part, **"Making the Most of the School Days,"** deals with those pre-college years, starting in middle school and continuing through high school. There is so much to be done when it comes to financial aid. What should you be doing—and when should you be doing it? How can you improve your situation, whatever it is? (Hint: It starts in middle school.)

2. Next, in **"Paying the Way,"** we'll move on to the actual application process and how to find and apply for every type of financial aid possible, including grants, scholarships, and loans. There are also work-study programs and other ways to defray the costs of college. How can you possibly understand and navigate it all? Don't worry. I've got you covered.

3. Finally, in **"Off and Away,"** we'll talk about how to give your student the financial skills they will need for life. Your college student needs to learn to manage money and stay on track with the plan you

have. We'll talk about how to manage college costs once your child is there. How do you keep them on track to graduate on time? I'll share my insights here as well.

This isn't going to be a step-by-step manual of what to do, because that information will become outdated as soon as this book goes into print. Instead, I'll give you the information you need to understand the process and point you in the right direction for each step. I will give you solid information and uncover resources you can use to most effectively and confidently find the answers that are applicable to your family situation. Where it's appropriate, I've included some charts, graphs, tips, and a worksheet or two to help you get the information you need in an easy-to-read, easy-to-understand format. In addition, you'll see some recurring elements throughout the book:

- **Good to Know:** Here you'll find smart tips and tidbits that many people don't know.
- **Let's Talk:** These talking points and scripts will help you with important conversations you need to have with your student.
- **The Bottom Line:** At the end of every chapter, we'll summarize key points in an easy-to-read format.

There's also a glossary to help you understand the "alphabet soup" of acronyms you'll come across. The book is designed for you to easily be able to refer to it, regardless of where you are in the process.

A FEW WORDS OF ADVICE

There's one other thing you should know about me: In addition to being a financial aid professional, I am the mother of two grown children, so I've been through this process from your perspective. Even with my experience in this area, going through it for our family was nerve-racking, so I get it.

I also feel like a mother to so many of my students who are nervously going through the college selection, application, and planning process. So, of course, it's my instinct to offer some motherly advice before we dive into the facts and process. Keep these four tips in mind to make the experience much easier on everyone involved.

1. **Take some time to celebrate the achievement.** I see so many people who are so focused on what is before them that they fail to take time to appreciate the great achievement their child has made. Graduating from high school is an accomplishment that should be celebrated! And now, your hard-working child is making plans for college. You have thought about this day since this young man or woman was a baby in your arms. You have a right to be proud. Let your child know how you feel about their success instead of only focusing on what needs to be done next.

2. **Start as early as you can.** It's surprising how many families wait until a child is a senior in high school before they start making financial plans for college. They are severely limiting their options by taking such a shortsighted approach. The more information

you can acquire and the earlier you can gather it, the better off you will be when it comes to making decisions. Some families get stuck making poor financial choices when they put themselves on an unnecessarily short schedule and leave no time to look for other options. If you started thinking about the financial aspects of paying for college the minute you brought your newborn home from the hospital, you've got a great start. But if that's not the case, there are still options, but the sooner you start looking at them, the better.

3. **Involve your child in the process.** I've seen parents exclude their students from the financial decision-making process, then turn around and complain that their child doesn't understand anything about money! Your college-bound student excels at learning, and it is your responsibility to provide learning opportunities for life. Choices made now can affect your child as well as your whole family, and everyone involved should know the facts behind the decisions made. Having your child involved at each point along the way helps them understand what it means to be financially responsible.

4. **Discuss student loans early in the process.** You've probably seen headlines about the massive student loan debt some students carry. One reason behind this astonishingly high figure is that parents fail to have a "money talk" with their children before college. Make sure your college-bound child understands the amount of money that has been borrowed

in federal and private student loans, and who will be responsible for repaying those loans. Student loans, especially from the federal government, can have lifelong financial consequences if they are not repaid. Yet far too many students still take out the maximum amount of loans available and use the money for living expenses or spring break trips, instead of thinking about ways to earn more money.

Follow these tips, and I promise you that your financial life will be much easier.

KNOW THE FINANCIAL AID ORDER

There is a well-established order for college financial aid, and it's important to understand this completely to get the most out of the process for your child. First, maximize the amount of "free" money your child receives. This is money that does not have to be repaid and comes in the form of grants and scholarships from colleges, federal and state governments, and private resources. The goal is to minimize the amount of money your family will be required to pay out-of-pocket.

The next step is to pay as much money as is reasonably possible based on your family's financial situation. The less money you have to borrow from any source, the better off you will be. Many parents and grandparents establish college savings accounts and may even realize some tax benefits by doing so. It's "all hands on deck" time to find ways to earn extra money to pay for college. Parents may decide to work overtime, while the student may participate in a work-study program at the school or find part-time employment off campus. This additional income can be used to offset travel and living expenses so that money doesn't have to be borrowed to pay for everyday costs.

The final step is to borrow money with caution. When borrowing, first take advantage of student and parent loans that are available from the federal government, then look to private lenders if additional money is required. Try to avoid putting college expenses on a credit card, as revolving interest charges can add up quickly.

The Financial Aid 3-Step

To get the most out of the financial aid process, it's important you follow this well-established order.

Step 1: Maximize "free" money. Use scholarships, grants, and other awards that don't need to be paid back.

Step 2: Pay as much as you can out-of-pocket. This includes savings, contributions from parents and relatives, 529 savings plans, part-time jobs, and work-study programs.

Step 3: Borrow with caution. Maximize federal loans first, then use private student loans only if necessary.

IT'S ALL WORTH IT

It's a lot of work and money, but most parents and students I know feel that a college degree is well worth the effort. According to the National Center for Education Statistics, young adults between the ages of 25 and 34 with a bachelor's degree had average earnings of more than twice as much as those who didn't have a high school diploma ($48,500 vs. $23,900) and 62 percent more than those who completed high school ($48,500 vs. $30,000).[1] In addition, students often find that attending college helps them learn important critical thinking and life-management skills that are just as important as what they take away from classroom instruction. Parents can feel comfortable knowing that their son or daughter has the information and skills necessary to make wise choices in life.

I encourage you to spend some time discussing the financial aid process with your high school student and talking about all the aspects of attending college, including the financial components. You might be surprised at the insights your child has, and it's entirely possible that you may learn from each other.

Keep calm, and don't let fear get the best of you. Millions of people have been through this process and survived! Knowledge and information are your friends. That's why you've turned to me. I'm going to help you take one step at a time and keep asking questions until you have the answers you need to make the choices that are best for you.

Visit my website CollegeFinancialAidAdvisors.com— join our mailing list, and keep in touch with me there. As financial aid programs and policies change, I'll continue to bring you the latest information to make the process less confusing.

Now, let's demystify a few of those "secrets."

PART 1

MAKING THE MOST
OF THE SCHOOL DAYS

1

Yes, It Starts in Middle School

MY FRIEND JIM SOUNDED EXASPERATED. He had just gotten the tuition numbers for the private middle school his son wanted to attend. He was a longtime friend and was calling for some advice about whether it was "worth it."

His son, Jeremy, was an average student and was having some difficulty fitting in at his school. The combination led Jim and his wife, Sarah, to wonder whether Jeremy would be better off at the Thornton School, a private middle school in a nearby town. Thornton would give him the support he needed to achieve more academically—and it would get him away from some of the social issues he was facing at the public school. But then Jim said what was really on his mind.

"I never thought I'd be paying this kind of tuition for middle school. Then he'll probably go to private high school. How am I supposed to save for college?"

What Jim didn't realize is that wherever there is a tuition payment, there is usually financial aid available. As we chatted on the phone, he found a flier in the information package that explained how to apply for financial aid at the school. He had been too upset to notice it before. As he read it, he had more questions. Last year, both he and Sarah had worked full time. But a few months ago, Sarah had lost her job. The financial aid form required last year's tax returns, which wouldn't be accurate for evaluating their current financial situation.

Jim's concerns were real and all too common among parents who are thinking ahead about their children's education. While I don't like to see anxious parents, it's a sign that these are people who are thinking ahead and trying to make the best financial decisions for their families. There is no answer that is right for everyone, but there is an answer that is right for you.

The first thing you need to know about financial aid is that you should never assume anything. Some families assume it's too hard to apply, while others think the results aren't worth the effort. Some families think they earn too little money to afford college, while others think they earn too much to qualify for any financial aid at all. But there are just as many stories of students from wealthy families earning a "free ride" as there are of aid going to homeless teenagers and children of immigrants who are the first generation to go to college. There are so many variables involved in the process that it is best not to prejudge anything. Take your time, learn the system, follow the process, and you might be surprised at how much you have achieved by the time your student puts on a cap and gown for high school graduation.

STARTING IN MIDDLE SCHOOL

I indicated that financial planning for college begins in middle school. The truth is that it is better if you start much earlier. As soon as you bring your baby home from the hospital and start receiving gifts, you should be thinking about putting that money away for a college fund. A huge stumbling block for most families is that they wait until high school to even start thinking about paying for college, and that really puts severe limitations on what can be accomplished.

I'm not saying that you have to be obsessed with funding college during every minute of your child's life, but it should be there somewhere in your family's financial planning. Talk about it before your baby is born, and make sure you're on the same page about your expectations, like:

- Whether it's important to both of you that your child goes to college
- The type of school you'd like your child to attend
- Cost, especially in relation to your family's finances
- Whether it's acceptable to access student loans to pay for college and whose responsibility it will be to pay them back

Of course, you can only make so many decisions without knowing what the future brings. Your child will have some input into the decisions, through their preferences, academic performance, and other factors. But it's important for parents to explore these ideas together. If you think it's important to get into the best school possible and sacrifice everything you can to pay for it, but your partner thinks it's best to spend two years at a community college and then transfer to a four-year college to save money, you have some work to do before you'll reach a game plan that's acceptable to both of you. Once you reach an agreement, then you can create a plan to make it happen.

After you have a plan in place, review it once a year as your child grows and goes through elementary school. By the time they reach middle school, you can move the discussions up to twice a year and maybe four times a year once your child is a junior in high school. As soon as your child is old enough to understand—usually during the middle school years—start including them in the discussions. While some may worry that sharing financial information with your child is inappropriate, it actually gives them ownership in the process and helps manage expectations. By trusting your child with this information, they can see, in context, how much you are doing to make this dream come true.

Many financial planners talk about the long-term benefits of saving money, and that is especially true when it comes to saving for college. It might seem like you are only saving a little bit of money, but think about what it could add up to over 18 years. If you can afford to put just $25 a week into a college fund, and then add in any cash gifts your child receives for birthdays, holidays, and other occasions, you might be able to save more than you think (see "A Little Can Add Up to a Lot"). You may be able to use a tax-advantaged savings plan, or you can just put the money in a savings account.

A Little Can Add Up to a Lot

Let's say you start saving $100 per month when your child is born at a 5 percent return. The results by the time they reach age 18 can be astounding.

Year 1:	$1,232
Year 5:	$6,809
Year 10:	$15,499
Year 18:	$34,666

Now, add in any gifts or contributions by other family members, and you could have a hefty education fund by the time your child is ready to go to school.

Of course, this is just an example. Performance, fees, and other factors will affect returns, so you shouldn't expect a 5 percent return in all cases. Contact your financial planner to determine the best savings option for you and to discuss what can be expected in your individual situation.

Having a cash reserve can also ease money worries down the road. Let's say your child is eligible to attend a college where the cost of attendance (COA) is $30,000 per year. They manage to qualify for $25,000 per year in grants, scholarships, and financial assistance, but that still leaves you with a bill of at least $5,000 per year. Families who haven't been saving money on a regular basis find themselves trying to scramble to earn extra cash each year or taking on student loans to cover the difference. Student loans are definitely helpful in covering the gap between costs and financial aid, but they can take a long time to repay and end up costing a lot more in the long run when you take the interest expense into consideration. It's a little like the old saying of "pay me now or pay me later." Which would you rather do—try to save $100 a month for 18 years while your child is growing up, or pay much more every month in student loans for 10 to 25 years after graduation?

SHOULD YOU PAY FOR MIDDLE SCHOOL?

Now, back to my friend Jim. While many parents don't have to worry about financial aid for their middle school children, parents like Jim and Sarah have good reasons to consider private or parochial schools. In their case, they had academic and social reasons to want to move Jeremy. Other parents may like the quality of the private school better or may think that a private middle school will allow the student to get into a better high school, which may lead to a better college. There are many reasons people choose this route. And many of them have to learn early about the adventures of completing financial aid forms to help pay for it.

There are always so many choices—is it better to do this, or should we do that? The answer is that it depends. You'll need to get solid information on the exact financial aid process in your state, and then try to calculate the impact on your family in each situation. It may help to have a professional adviser on your side who can help guide you through this process. At each stage, you have to do what's best for your child. If life at one school is miserable, it's probably a good idea to find another school. Some private schools offer additional support to struggling students. And yet the tuition may take a bite out of what you can save for college. Each issue raises tough questions.

One thing I always tell my families is that it is never too early or too late to look for scholarships. Most people only associate this process with applying to college, but there are scholarships available for students in elementary, middle, and high school. Once your child is in college, the scholarship process shouldn't end either, as there are some that don't even kick in until a student is a college sophomore or junior.

Starting to Save

One of the most important things you can do for your child's college education is to open a 529 savings plan. The federal government allows you to save money for education and the earnings to grow tax-free. States have different tax regulations, so it's also a good idea to check in with your accountant about state taxation and any other financial impact.

The best fund for you will vary depending on your family's circumstances. I'm not a financial planner, but here are three great places to get more information:

- **IRS.gov:** That's right. The IRS will give you information about 529 savings plans and how they work, as well as restrictions on using the money for anything other than education-related expenses.
- **Savingforcollege.com:** This comprehensive website discusses various savings strategies and options.
- **CollegeFinancialAidAdvisors.com:** For more information about the financial aid process, you can also visit my website.

LAYING THE FOUNDATION FOR SUCCESS

Middle school is the time to get your child thinking about college and whether that's the right path for them. That way, you can start doing some financial planning. You might think it's a little too early to start thinking about college. After all, this is your baby! And while you don't want to start pressuring your student to have the rest of their life figured out—since many of us don't even have that done 20 or 30 years later—now is the time to lay the foundation for a successful academic future. So, no, it's not too early to start.

Your child's middle school years should include a taste of independence—for better or for worse. Teachers and guidance counselors typically encourage parents to take a step back and let their students learn how to take more responsibility for things like homework, grades, and even advocating for themselves in class. Now is the time to let your student work out concerns with a teacher and take responsibility for keeping a schedule of assignments and tests in an age- and ability-appropriate way. You might even—gasp—let your student feel the bad-grade consequences of not doing the work. That's a tough one, but better to learn that lesson now than when it will drag down a high-school GPA, which might catch an admissions officer's eye.

Of course, all this happens under your watchful eye, and you are free to intervene when needed. But when your student gets into high school, the expectations and schoolwork are going to ramp up. It will be easier for your student to handle that if you've let them get some practice, including:

- **Foster good study habits.** Your middle school student will be challenged in new ways. Learning how to carve out time for studying, projects, and writing is important to get the best possible grades. Encourage your student to think ahead and look at upcoming assignments, quizzes, and tests to plan a study routine. The study habits formed now will help them throughout their academic life.

- **Get to know the school's system.** Some schools encourage working with teachers while others prefer that student questions and concerns be handled through the guidance counselor. Get to know how to best address your student's needs and get feedback about areas where they are struggling or excelling. Some schools group students by academic aptitude early on, so you'll want to be aware of whether your student is being identified appropriately according to their aptitude. Keeping in touch with contacts at the school is a good way to stay on top of what's happening with your child.

- **Encourage community involvement and leadership roles.** Throughout their school years and beyond, your student is going to be judged in part by how they take on leadership roles. When you encourage simple actions—serving in a club or taking on responsibility for a school fundraiser—early on, these become natural to the student and help develop an impressive resume by the time they start filling out college applications. When involvement and leadership are encouraged from a young age, it's not a chore to get involved later.

As long as you're not putting tremendous pressure on your child to start worrying about college in sixth grade, helping them learn these life skills is a good thing. It will also help them throughout the rest of their schooling—and even their lives. We all need to be able to learn new things when it's necessary and be active, engaged members of our community. Middle school is as good a time to start as any.

THINKING ABOUT THE FUTURE

Try to get an idea about potential career interests, talk about what is important in campus life, find out whether your child is thinking in-state or out-of-state, small or large, urban or rural, in terms of campus locations. You can peruse websites together and talk about what appeals to your child and what doesn't sound all that interesting. Perhaps you can take some time during a family vacation to stop by a college just to get a feel for the campus. Maybe you could even put a "dream board" together with pictures of potential schools that can serve as a constant motivator for your child. The secret is that this will also be giving you some insight into what the costs may be to send your child to a particular school. That way, you can make sure your savings keep up with the goal. If a particular school comes up as an all-time favorite and your child isn't swayed over the course of several years, you might even want to investigate the possibility of prepaid tuition.

State-run prepaid tuition programs are a form of 529 savings plans that allow you to "lock in" tuition credits at rates slightly above today's average rates, presumably saving money over the long haul as tuitions increase. They can be redeemed to pay for college credits when your child is ready to go to college. While they aren't typically subject to market volatility like fund-based 529 plans, they do have risks. Many have closed down in recent years, and, according to Bankrate.com, some experts believe they will be nonexistent in the coming years.[2] There may also be restrictions on how they are used. Check with your financial planner to explore the risks.

LET'S TALK

Future Plans

Sometimes, nothing makes a child shut down faster than asking, "What do you want to be when you grow up?" It's a big question, and, really, who the heck knows at age 11 or 12? To gauge interests, try asking these questions instead:

● What was your favorite thing that you did today?

● If you could do anything in the world right now, what would it be?

Keep your child involved in the process, and it will seem like just another normal family activity. If your child lands a summer job or some type of part-time employment, discuss how much of that income should go into the college fund. This will give them more of a vested interest in doing well in high school and going on to college.

THE BOTTOM LINE

- If you haven't started one already, open a 529 savings plan. Each state has different rules when it comes to these plans, so be sure to consult your financial planner before making any moves.
- Lay the foundation for future success by helping students develop good study habits, get involved in the community, and take on leadership roles.
- Start talking about college, as well as possible interests and strengths for the future.

Planning through the High School Years

JANE AND STAN GOODWIN HAD TWO DAUGHTERS in high school. Elise was going into her senior year, and Chelsea was entering her freshman year. In short, when they came to see me, they were panicked. Elise was a great student and was looking at some of the most expensive schools in the country to begin her pre-med studies. Chelsea was less driven, with average grades and no idea what she wanted to do.

The Goodwins had $20,000 saved in each daughter's 529 plan, but the true cost of having two children in college—especially two students with such divergent academic styles—was worrying them. Should they let Elise go to the best school she could get into, regardless of the cost? Then, did they need to offer the same opportunity to Chelsea? How could they let each daughter maximize her potential, but still be fair to both?

The Goodwins realized they were a bit late to the game in just starting to plan for Elise's college education, but they had more time to plan for Chelsea's. They needed to make the most of the time they had left before each daughter was packing the car to head to college.

Today's college-track high school students are typically a busy, active bunch. They may be balancing schoolwork with a couple of sports teams, music programs, clubs, community service, and a part-time job. Of course, you don't want to put more pressure on them, but it's time to start thinking about the years after high school. Here is a year-by-year game plan that can help you and your student tackle everything that needs to be done in an orderly way.

A FRESHMAN ALREADY?!

When did that happen? Your baby was just crawling on the floor yesterday and is now heading to high school? Time certainly does fly, especially when you are raising children. Now, it seems like there is so much more to cram into those four short years, and it somehow doesn't seem as if there is enough time to get everything done.

Freshman year is a time of transition. Your child is getting used to the rigors of high school while figuring out everything from their locker combination to how to meet the demands of their coursework. They may be going to school with unfamiliar classmates and making new friends. In some cases, this may be the first time your child has had to change classes, take responsibility for their schoolwork, or figure out how to balance clubs, sports, schoolwork and, perhaps, a part-time job.

At the same time your student is adapting to all these changes and firmly on the path toward adulthood, it can feel like it's too much to add college planning to the mix. After all, there's plenty of time, right?

Well, yes and no. You don't need to begin pressuring your child to have a college, major, and life plan figured out before the senior-year homecoming football game. But it's definitely time to start encouraging your child to think about the future so you can take the time you have left and plan accordingly. Here are some of the key goals for freshman year.

- **Solidify your studies.** Do you remember those study habits we discussed helping your children develop in middle school? Now, they're even more important. Help your student have the confidence to seek extra help if certain subjects become a challenge. Tutors, teachers' extra help sessions, and peers can all offer your student assistance in shoring up weaker areas.
- **Get involved.** If your child isn't already involved in extracurricular activities and community service, this is a great time to start. High school typically offers a range of options based on a student's interests. From sports or foreign language clubs to high school publications and student government, encourage your child to use these options to explore their interests. Such extras can also look great on

college applications, especially if your student takes on leadership roles.

- **Write down activities and achievements.** It's too hard to look back over four years and try to remember everything your child will want to include on college applications. Instead, just start a word processing document, file, or notebook, and encourage your child to log or file reminders, awards, and other remembrances as they go along. Dust it off at application time, and you will have a clear record of accomplishments.
- **Think about references.** Your child might have really hit it off with a teacher, found a great coach, or worked with a wonderful mentor. You make a mental note that the person could provide a great reference, but, when your child goes back to ask for it, the person has moved on or retired from teaching, and it's too late. It's never inappropriate to ask for a letter of reference from these people while their interaction with your child is still fresh in their minds. They also won't be under the time pressures that most reference writers are and can make sure their letter truly reflects the relationship they had with your child.
- **Start thinking about colleges.** It's too much to expect a junior or senior to review thousands of college opportunities and pick a few while keeping up with everything else at school. Start talking about different types of colleges and their benefits and programs. You might even start visiting a few

schools to let your freshman know what it feels like to be on a college campus.

- **Introduce the money conversation.** Your child should be able to make smart financial decisions in life, and learning how to budget for a major expense like going to college can be a very worthwhile learning experience. Give your child a budget to manage—either money you give through an allowance or money they earn through work. Communicate your expectations about your child's contribution and what you expect them to save for college.

DON'T SLIP INTO THE SOPHOMORE SLUMP!

By sophomore year, your student is likely going to be settled in to school and feel more at home. With a year of experience under their belt, your student knows the school layout cold, has found a new batch of friends and interests, and is probably also surrounded by people who are starting to think seriously about school and their areas of study. Use this momentum to your advantage to continue some of the conversations you've started—and to put some new plans in place.

- **Hone interests.** Your student likely has several activities they enjoy. Discuss possible areas of study or those that seem interesting as a profession. If you have contacts who can take your child to work for a day so they can see what the job is like, even better. Students may also look for part-time jobs or even internships or community service opportunities in their areas of interest. Knowing what they want to do will play an important role in college selection.

- **Keep working on the college list.** Spend time with your student continuing to explore and refine the college list. The goal is to narrow down the list of possible schools to about 10 that are well-regarded for the subject they want to study. You might help your student create a chart or spreadsheet so all of you can compare costs, potential earnings after graduation, and personal preferences. For example, does your student want to go to a big school with a robust sports program or a smaller school that might have smaller class sizes and more personalized attention?

As you learn more about your student's preferences, you'll add and subtract schools from the list. Visit some of them, when possible, or attend an open house for those that may be near you. Look at the admissions requirements and start thinking about what your child might need to do to get into their top schools. Familiarize yourself with essay topics, and have your child jot down ideas that could be developed more when the time comes. Students interested in certain majors might need to develop portfolios and should definitely be working on this the whole time they are in high school.

- **Set new savings goals.** As you discuss the financial realities of college with your student, you should also help them set savings goals. From gifts of cash to part-time job earnings, your child should be setting aside a portion of every check to the college fund. It's important to help them manage expenses now because in a few short years, they will be off at college, where savvy money management will be expected. Every dime saved is that much less you need to find or borrow.

Look at PSATs—Stat!

Consider having your child take the Preliminary SAT/National Merit Scholarship Qualifying Test (PSAT/NMSQT) during their sophomore year. The test, which is administered by the College Board, will give your child some experience in taking such a test. That can help quell nerves when it's time for the SAT. In addition, taking the PSAT can help your child qualify for a National Merit Scholarship and give you an indicator of whether or not you should do some pre-SAT tutoring or classes to strengthen your child's test-taking aptitude.

JUNIOR YEAR—IT'S NO JOKE

Junior year is where the rubber really starts to meet the road in the letters I receive from parents. Some seem to be on the right track and just need some general guidance or advice, while others have already worked themselves into panic mode. Should we make any financial moves now? We're getting divorced and haven't been able to work out the finances yet—how will this affect our child's future? We haven't saved any money yet—what should we do? While there are no simple answers to any of these questions, the good news is that there are always actions you can take to make the situation better.

This third year of high school can be quite a tumultuous time. While grades were always important, they become much more so now. The joy of being one step closer to your student's high school graduation goal can be offset by the trepidation of not knowing what lies down the path to getting into college—or how you're going to pay for it. Some families get themselves too worried about the process, while others seem to think that not worrying about it will somehow make it go away.

The junior year should be looked at as the springboard to the college-bound process. The academic year runs from August or September through May or June, depending on where you live. This is important for academic progress, extracurricular activities, college admission tests, financial aid, and narrowing down college choices.

Most parents will be able to file a Free Application for Federal Student Aid (FAFSA) in October of their child's senior year. Depending on the school, some parents may need to file a College Scholarship Service (CSS) Profile around the same time.

The junior year is important because it is probably your student's last chance to make a good impression before starting the college application process during senior year. Here are some of the things juniors should be doing in their college search.

- **Get into detail about finances.** You've been talking about college and the importance of saving, but now it's time to get into specifics before your child has their heart set on a school that's financially out of reach. I say that with a caveat. I see many parents who automatically rule out certain schools, especially private ones, before they have all the facts. Most schools have a cost of attendance (COA) that they publish, which includes tuition, room and board, fees, books, and other expenses. Sometimes, those numbers can make you feel like you're going to faint. But private schools may have bigger wells of money for merit and other forms of aid that they can give. It's not a "sure thing," but what you really need to look at is the percentage of students who receive financial aid and what the average aid award is. There are times when that pricey private school can actually cost you less than your state university!

You may find that the generalities you discussed early on were subject to different interpretations. It's only fair to your student to make it clear how much you can pay toward their education. I've seen situations where parents expected their students to pay for most or all of their college through aid and loans. Your child needs to know such financial expectations sooner rather than later.

- **Narrow down the college list.** By the beginning of your child's junior year, they should have a list of roughly 10 to 20 colleges that fit their general requirements. Your student should find a way that is comfortable for them to start saving information on these schools. Some students like to put a big chart on the wall so they can visually see how the colleges compare against each other. Other students like to keep notes on their computers. Some just like to have a notebook or folder where they can write and file their thoughts or questions as they come up, so they can refer to them later when they have additional time. Help your child find the way that works best for them before the information becomes overwhelming, and you find yourself not being able to remember which college has the liberal arts program and which one has the study abroad opportunity your son or daughter liked. The goal is to slowly whittle those colleges down to 5 to 10 by the end of the junior year so your student can make some decisions on where they want to apply their senior year.

- **Make campus visits.** Now is the time to start making those road trips to college campuses. Begin thinking about when you might be able to schedule visits to a few of your child's top schools, and encourage them to talk to classmates and accompany them on campus visits. Seeing a campus not only gives your student a feel for whether the school is a good fit, but it also starts helping your student understand what they want—and don't want—in a college experience. Talk to your child about what they want to see and who they want to talk to, and the questions you and your student want to ask. It is crucial that you spend time with the financial aid office during your visit. Be prepared to ask questions and have a way to keep track of the answers you receive. Ask about the average COA and the typical amount of financial aid for all four years, as well as living expenses and how much student loan debt the average graduate

College Questions? Check!

Keep this checklist of important questions handy for college visits.

☐ What is your overall graduation rate? What percentage of students graduate in four years? In five years?

☐ What are the biggest obstacles to graduating in four years?

☐ What percentage of students in my major have a job within six months of graduation? Within a year?

☐ What is the average starting salary for students in my major?

☐ What is the average financial aid package?

☐ What percentage of financial need does the school typically meet?

☐ What is the typical percentage of loans vs. grants or scholarships?

☐ What is the average student loan debt of last year's graduates?

☐ What is the average class size of introductory classes? Of more specialized classes?

☐ What are the housing accommodations for freshmen? Which residence is the most popular with students?

☐ What resources are available for students who need help with coursework?

☐ What other support services are available to students?

☐ What is student life like? What activities, clubs, and other organizations are strong on campus?

☐ What is the best part of going to school here? What is the worst?

Add your own questions here:

☐ _____

☐ _____

☐ _____

☐ _____

has. Find out how many students leave after the first or second semester, how many graduate, and how many students typically graduate from that school in four years. Then, ask how many of their graduates get jobs in their field of study and how much those jobs typically pay. This is all information the school should have on hand and that will help you and your child make solid financial choices later.

- **Be a resume coach.** Just like you need to prepare a resume for a job interview, your student needs a good resume to impress their intended schools. If your child's academic record has been less than stellar, work with them to make a concerted effort this year to improve their grades. It's important to try to find activities or leadership roles to show off interests and abilities. College also looks for students who give back to their communities through service and volunteerism. These activities can also be experiences that will broaden your student's horizons, prepare them for the college experience, and make your child a well-rounded student who would be an asset to any college's student body. Look for activities that represent your child's interests. Some activities that may have an impact on college admissions officers include:

  - Student government
  - Student media, such as a school newspaper or television station
  - Clubs or groups where your student takes on increasing leadership responsibility

- ○ Sports
- ○ Volunteering with nonprofits or charitable efforts
- ○ Self-directed initiatives, such as a campaign, drive, or effort that the student began themselves.

But, really, any activity can be considered important if it showcases your child's skills and interests. It's part of the patchwork that shows the kind of individual you've raised, so don't try to force an activity that isn't a good fit just because it "looks good." Ultimately, what matters is that your child shows an interest in the world and in developing themselves as a person.

- **Prepare for admissions tests.** This is also the time when your child will need to start thinking about the college admissions tests. Check the websites of your child's preferred colleges to find out if they require the SAT or ACT, or if they accept either test. Some colleges have even moved away from this requirement and are developing a holistic approach to applying for college, which places less emphasis on test results and formal applications, and more on students' ability to demonstrate their unique capabilities. It is always wise to find out exactly what is required for each college. Then, visit the test administrators' websites and find out what is involved in each. For many students, test prep courses, like the Khan Academy's free SAT test prep, can be a good idea to help them learn how to take these exams and gain greater confidence in taking such a long test. Your child may also want to take practice tests or study courses, based on their academic abilities, before taking the actual test. Find out when the tests are administered, and be sure your child leaves enough time to study, take the test, and take it again if necessary, before the college application process begins.

- **Keep saving money.** The one thing that always seems to surprise the parents of college freshmen to whom I speak is the amount of out-of-pocket expenses college students have. If your student is living on campus, you might be amazed at all the little things you took for granted at home: toiletries, morning coffee, late-night pizza runs, pens, memory sticks, snacks, and the list goes on. You and your student should try to save as much money as you can while they are in high school so your child won't have to rely on credit cards or student loans to cover living expenses at college.

Have your child help you calculate potential college, book, and living expenses, and compare that against the money that has been saved. Then discuss what else might need to be done to make up any dollar shortfalls. Have an honest conversation about the benefits and negatives of credit. Show your child that people who don't have a solid plan in place for repaying money that is borrowed could be setting themselves up for lifelong financial difficulties.

There are definitely a lot of things to think about during the junior year of high school, let alone waiting for junior prom to come around! By then it's May and June and, before you know it, your little child is a senior in high school!

Your Top 10

Your top 10 list will likely change, but use a list similar to this, for each school that is appealing to you.

Name of School _____

Location (City/State) _____

What You Like About It _____

_____

_____

_____

Type of School (e.g., big or small, public or private, etc.) _____

Concerns _____

_____

_____

Cost _____

Average Financial Aid Award _____

Best Majors Offered _____

_____

Student Life (clubs, sports, fraternities and sororities, or other desired offerings) _____

_____

Companies that Recruit Here _____

_____

_____

_____

THE BOTTOM LINE

- Set goals for each year and assign timelines to them. Check in on the deadlines you've set for yourself at least monthly.
- Connect with your child's guidance counselor and address any academic issues early on.
- Attend college fairs at your high school or in your community and meet with representatives.
- Check the high school calendar for college nights or financial aid night.
- Start working on your child's top 10 schools list.
- Go on campus visits and attend local college fairs to get a good idea of what various schools offer.
- Stay calm! You've got this!

How Can Seniors Get It All Done?

ALEX, THE ASSOCIATE DIRECTOR OF MY COMPANY, told me that Sally Morgan was on the phone. I remembered her from a year ago when she had called with a question about her son's FAFSA form. She wanted to know the best time to hire me to help her with the financial aid process. Initially, she thought that hiring me the spring of her son's senior year would give her enough time. However, once we started going over everything she needed to get done before her son even started his senior year, she soon changed her mind.

Usually, it's best if I start working with families during the spring of the student's junior year in high school. That way, I have a few months during the school year before their senior year to help the student tie up any loose ends and advise the family about what should be done to give their student the best chances of application success. (Even though I'm not an admissions counselor, I've picked up a few tips along the way.) Starting near the end of their junior year also gives us the summer to work together and stay on track, plowing through that big to-do list!

Senior year brings a mix of emotions. It's the moment you and your child have been waiting for, on the cusp of adulthood and getting ready to head off to college and start life's next chapter. It can be exhilarating, with so much to do and so much promise for the future. But it can also be frightening, with so many questions.

- How do we get everything done?
- What if we do something wrong?
- How will we pay for college?

Suddenly, it seems like time is flying by too quickly and there just aren't enough hours in the day. Take a deep breath. Here's how you'll get it all done.

THE SUMMER BEFORE SENIOR YEAR IS HARD WORK!

There aren't any lazy days of summer for rising seniors. Yes, you want your child to have some fun before senior year, but you want them to get some things done, too, so their senior year isn't too crazy. Work with your child to set aside a specific amount of time each week to work on the college process. Treat it like a summer class, and plan assignments and deadlines that need to be met. That way, you won't be overwhelmed when September rolls around and it's time to juggle schoolwork on top of the college application process.

In addition to part-time work and activities, your soon-to-be senior will have a busy few months preparing for what's ahead. You used your child's freshman, sophomore, and junior year to lay the groundwork to get them ready to apply to, and pay for, college, so by this point in high school, they should:

- Be prepared to rattle off a top 10 list of college possibilities—and have visited at least a few.
- Understand the application requirements for their favorite schools.
- Have taken or be getting ready to take the SAT or ACT exam.
- Have a list of scholarship possibilities, complete with deadlines and submission needs.

If you haven't done any of this work yet, don't panic. There's still time. You just have a busy summer ahead of you!

STARTING THE APPLICATION PROCESS

Your child has compiled a list of their top schools and the deadlines for application. Those deadlines will vary, depending on the type of decision your child is seeking. Yes, that's right—there are different types of admission decisions you can expect from a school, and you'll want to get to know these terms to avoid confusion.

- **Early action:** This is a good choice for students who have two or three top schools and are relatively confident they'll be admitted, based on their test scores and grades. Early action is basically applying for a quicker decision—some schools open applications as early as August with decisions as early as mid-December. Early action is nonbinding—your son or daughter can still apply to as many colleges as they wish and will often have until the regular admission deadline to make a decision. It just helps alleviate the anxiety of waiting to know if you got into your top schools.

Consider this option if: Your student has a few top choices they are likely to get into and wants quick decisions and to compare offers without making any commitments.

- **Single choice early action:** This is similar to early action in that it results in an early, nonbinding decision, but you can only apply to one college. The benefit here is that your child is signaling to the school that it's their number-one choice. From an admissions perspective, that's attractive: Colleges are competing for the best students. If they want to offer you a spot and you've indicated you'll likely take it, you're apt to be more attractive to them.

  Consider this option if: Your student has one top college and is likely to make the cut, but doesn't want the decision to be binding.

- **Early decision:** Early decision is often confused with early action, *but there is a very important difference.* Early decision is binding, which means that if your child is accepted, they must withdraw all applications to other schools as long as the family can afford the financial aid package. So, there are no do-overs. Your student can only apply for early decision to one school— any other school applications must be regular decision. However, there are a couple of other considerations when it comes to applying early decision. First, it may sometimes hurt your chances of negotiating for more financial aid. With early decision, since the decision is binding, you'll receive a letter that requires you to withdraw from other institutions. The letter might have wording that indicates you may be excused from doing so if the financial aid package isn't sufficient.

However, with early decision, you'll be at a disadvantage when it comes to comparing financial aid packages, since you'll likely need to formalize your commitment before you even get offers from other schools. Bottom line: If your child has a "dream college" and wants to go there if accepted, no matter what, this may be an option. If your child meets admission criteria, you're sending a commitment to the school that your child will attend. Since schools want to accept eligible students who will attend, this may be an advantage. Deadlines for early decision are usually in November, with notification by mid-December.

Consider this option if: Your child has a dream school to which they are likely to be accepted, and your family is prepared to commit to the school and withdraw all other applications.

- **Regular admission:** This is your good, old-fashioned application process. This deadline can vary, depending on the college, but usually falls somewhere between January 1 and February 1, although some schools have regular decision deadlines as early as November 1, so it's important to be familiar with each school's deadlines. It is advisable to have your essays written and your recommendations in line by the end of November so you don't get caught in a holiday rush. Acceptance notices are sent out between March and April.

Consider this option if: Your child has several schools to which they want to apply and is open to choosing from among the best options in terms of admission offers and financial aid.

- **Rolling admission:** Schools that have this type of admission policy simply review all applications as they are received and notify students on an ongoing basis. This can be good if you want to apply to a certain college to see if you have a chance at being accepted and still want to leave yourself time to apply to others if you aren't accepted.

Consider this option if: The school you love has a rolling admission policy.

GOOD TO KNOW

Don't Be Fooled by Early Decision Stats

Some schools may report that a large percentage of their class is early decision in order to pressure you into applying that way, but these statistics can be deceiving. Very often, many of those students are athletes who will be attending on a scholarship basis. Don't fall for the pressure tactic!

GIVE YOURSELF THE GIFT OF TIME

Here's a blast of the obvious: Applying to college can be a time-consuming process. Of course, we know that, but procrastination is a powerful factor, especially when it comes to the preparation that needs to be done for school applications.

Be sure you understand the admissions process at each school. Hundreds of schools accept the Common Application, also called the Common App, which allows you to fill out one application and forward it to participating schools to which you want to apply. Some schools take the Common App alone, while others may use the Common App with extra requirements or information. Others have their own process entirely. It can be confusing to track the requirements of each school, so work with your student to develop a way to track what they need to do for each top choice.

Completing the application requires more than just putting information in form boxes. In addition to the application itself, your child may have to write at least one essay and, possibly, include a video, portfolio, or other type of information or backup. Your child may also need transcripts or recommendations forwarded to the school. Depending on whether your child is applying for early admission, early decision, or regular admission, your deadlines will vary. It's best to work on and finalize essay requirements at least a couple of months before the deadline—more if your child has trouble writing. Plan on submitting the application at least two weeks prior to the deadline—you will want to leave yourself a little wiggle room, just in case something doesn't go according to plan. It's usually best to apply as soon as you can.

It's a good idea to make a list of what needs to be completed by your target date and then work backward to develop your schedule. How long do you think it will take your child to complete everything? Two months might not be unrealistic if you want to leave yourselves time to request references and transcripts, polish essays, or tweak an application. This means that students trying for early action applications must begin the process by mid-August at the latest and may be trying to get their transcripts just as their senior year is starting. Yikes!

Take my word for it when I tell you that it's never too early to start preparing for the application. Give your student plenty of time so the process is less stressful.

LET'S TALK

Getting the Application Done

Time is flying by and no matter what you do, it seems impossible to get your student to complete those college applications. This can be a big source of conflict.

Try to find out if there's a reason behind the procrastination. Maybe the process is intimidating or confusing to your student and they don't know how to proceed. Perhaps there is some trepidation about moving from high school into college. Or maybe it's simply a time management issue, and your student is having trouble fitting in applications between all the other things that need to be done their senior year.

The one thing you don't want is to do the application for your student. Admissions officers can spot a parent-written essay a mile away. This is an important responsibility that your child needs to complete. They may just need your guidance and support through the process.

Application Prep List

Before your student sits down to complete the application, they should be prepared. They will need:

- High school transcripts to be sent to their schools of choice
- Background information about parents or guardians, including date(s) of birth, education background, employer contact information, etc.
- List of extracurricular activities, such as sports, clubs, and volunteer work, including activities outside of school
- List of awards, honors, and other distinctions
- SAT and/or ACT scores
- Completed essay for each school

Each application may have different information requirements, so your student should be sure to find out what other information is needed to make the best use of their time.

FILLING OUT THE APPLICATION

Applications vary, but most ask for the basic information like name, address, telephone number, and email address. They'll also ask for the student's academic background and transcripts, as well as the parents' or guardians' educational backgrounds. You should provide your student with your employer's name and contact information, since they'll likely need that too. Your student should also be prepared to answer questions about their interests and intended areas of study.

One of the most intimidating parts of the application for many students is the essay or personal statement. This written portion of the application helps the college get a sense of the student's writing style and how they think. It's often the written version of "tell me about yourself" in an interview. Encourage your student to be authentic. Let their interests and personality shine. An admissions officer may only spend a minute or two reading the essay, so it should start off strong and show them why the student would be a good addition to the school. Oh—and I can't stress this enough—make sure your student proofreads the essay! This is where you might be able to lend a second set of eyes to spot typos or misspellings. But don't edit it heavily or rewrite it. Aside from the ethics issues, it's important that this statement be in your student's own voice.

KNOW THE SCORE IN ADMISSIONS TESTS

Another important item to go on the application prep list is your admissions test score. The most common admissions tests are the SAT and ACT, both of which used to have "formal" names but are referred to only by their acronyms now. Most colleges will accept either test, and some are even test-optional, but be sure you know which test your child's preferred schools require.

The SAT is administered by the College Board and measures aptitude, while the ACT measures achievement. In other words, the SAT is more focused on your critical thinking and reasoning skills, while the ACT is more about the knowledge you've acquired in the classroom. The SAT was recently changed to emphasize words in context and to give real-world context to the problems you consider during the test. The scoring also changed to a different model. If you want to explore these changes and find out more information about the SAT, visit collegereadiness.collegeboard.org/sat.

Here is where your student can use the test differences to their advantage. Let's say your child is good at figuring out problems and writes well. The SAT may be the better test, since it has an essay section and allows some of that reasoning ability to shine through. On the other hand, if your child is better at memorizing and retaining classroom work, the ACT may be the better bet. Of course, your student can take both and let the test scores make the decision.

While preparing for the test, find at least two dates when each test is administered in your area prior to your application deadline, and add their registration deadlines to your student's calendar. Your child's guidance counselor may be able to help with this. It's a good idea to have a primary date and a backup date in case your child decides to take the test a second time to try to improve their score. Many students do this, especially because it's common to be nervous the first time they take it.

Should your child take the test a second time? Many students take the test once in their junior year and once in the fall of their senior year. But research shows that multiple test tries can improve scores. Since you send your best score to the school, the only thing your student has to lose is the additional registration fee.

If your student is nervous about the test, there are many test preparation classes and books, including free resources offered through the test websites:

- **SAT practice (collegereadiness.collegeboard.org/ sat/practice):** Resources here include a free question of the day, which is a great way to prep over time by working on one question each day. In addition, you'll find other sample questions and a practice test you can take for free. There are also other affordable study aids.

- **ACT practice (www.act.org/content/act/en/ products-and-services/the-act/test-preparation. html):** This site also has a free question of the day, as well as sample questions and tests, an affordable digital test prep kit, and other resources.

Your child's school may also offer study resources and help. In addition, there are many commercial tutors and classes available. To find the best in your area, get suggestions from your school guidance counselor and ask other parents for referrals.

What Happens When Students Take the SAT and ACT Again?

ACT[3]

- 57% increased their score
- 21% had no change
- 22% scored lower

SAT[4]

- 55% of juniors increased their scores as seniors
- 10% had no change
- 35% scored lower

It's not possible to "cram" for the ACT or SAT. Start tackling sample questions and tests at least a few months prior to get comfortable with the types of questions asked and get help in areas where your student may be weak.

GOOD TO KNOW

Come Prepared to the ACT or SAT

Your child will need to bring certain supplies to the test. In addition to getting a good night's sleep the night before the test and having a good breakfast, make sure you know what your student will need for the test, including plenty of sharpened pencils, type of calculator, and photo identification.

MY APPLICATION IS IN—NOW WHAT?

It's great that your student was able to plan the work, and work the plan. Once the applications are in, the waiting begins. But that doesn't mean your student has nothing left to do. Keep these things in mind.

- **Clean up social media.** Today, many colleges look at your student's social media pages as a part of the admissions process. Don't risk turning off an admissions officer because of off-color or questionable social media content. Students have lost scholarships, been kicked out of fraternities and sororities, or met other consequences because of poor judgment in a photo, tweet, or post.

  Some of the more popular social media platforms are Instagram and Twitter. Snapchat is a social media app where the images sent disappear after a few seconds, but can also be saved as "stories." Other popular social media platforms include Facebook, YouTube, and Pinterest. Make sure all your son or daughter's social media platforms are made private so that only people they approve can see posts, and be sure anything questionable is removed. Try to put yourself in the place of a college admissions officer, responsible for deciding whether a student should attend their college. Swearing, drinking, smoking, pranks, and other questionable behavior may be fun among friends, but they definitely don't make you look like good college material.

- **Follow up.** It's important that your student follows up with the schools to which they applied to be sure that they received all parts of their application, as well as transcripts, midyear grade reports, and copies of admissions test scores. Be sure to respond to any of the college's or university's requests for information immediately.

- **Schedule an interview.** Some schools like to interview students. They may send an alumni or school representative to your area to meet with the student and get a sense of their personality and interests. In some cases, the school may be close enough that the interview can be done there. If your student interacts well with people, an interview can be a good idea.

- **Skip the senioritis.** Your child might feel like it's time to cut loose and have a little fun, but going too far could be a problem. A sudden slide in grades, dropping extracurricular activities, or a suspension can all attract the attention of college admissions officers. Grades still matter. Colleges have the ability to rescind an offer, and they have been known to use it. This could put your student in a real bind trying to find another college on such short notice.

That's not to say your student can't have a little fun. It's the last year of high school, and it should be a time of making memories with friends while preparing for this exciting new chapter. Your child should enjoy activities and spend quality time with friends and family. Graduation day will be here before you know it.

A Sample Application Timeline

These are the typical steps in the application process. You and your student can use this sample timeline as a guideline to create your own.

August

- Request application and information from colleges.
- Visit school campuses throughout the fall to help narrow the choices.
- Look into overnight or weekend college visitation programs.
- Make plans to stay with friends who are in college in the fall.
- Create a schedule of admissions and financial aid deadlines.

September

- Senior year starts!
- Mark your calendar for college fairs and admissions representatives' visits.
- Suggest that your student meet with the school counselor to develop a college admissions plan.
- Register for the SAT or the ACT. Investing in a preparation course for either test may help your student become more comfortable with the testing process and perform better on the exam.

October

- Begin completing college applications and essays.
- Request transcripts and letters of recommendation.

- Explore college scholarship information.
- Suggest your student meet with a guidance counselor if they plan to apply for early action or early decision.
- Complete Free Application for Federal Student Aid (FAFSA), which has a new deadline. More on this in Chapter 5, "How Does All This Work, Anyway?"
- Complete and submit the CSS Profile, which goes live on October 1.

November

- Follow up to ensure that letters of recommendation are submitted.
- Complete essays and applications.
- Submit college applications for early decision/early action programs for any college with November deadlines.

December

- Obtain any other supplemental financial aid forms that may be required by your target schools.
- Check that the school administrator has sent the transcript and recommendation(s) to each school to which your child is applying.
- Receive admissions notification(s) from early action and early decision schools.

January

- If attending early action or early decision schools, rescind admissions applications from other colleges.
- Continue applying for scholarships.

February

- If your student applied early decision or early action and was deferred, they should talk to their guidance counselor about updating their application.
- Your student should make sure the school administrator sent colleges their semester grades.
- Check to see that all your application materials have been sent.
- If your student is taking any college entrance exams, they should check the dates they'll be taking their first and second SATs and ACTs.

March

- Your student should ask their high school counselor about Advanced Placement (AP) exams offered for college credit and about the cost of the exams. They should contact the registrar's office at the college or school they plan to attend to find out what score is necessary to receive the college credit. If your student will be taking an AP exam, they should consider starting an AP preparation course for the tests in May.
- Receive admissions notification(s).

April

- Receive admissions notification(s).
- Your student should notify schools they have chosen not to attend, but have been accepted to, that they will not be attending.
- If you and your student can, attend college admit day or a regional admit day in your state for the school of their choice.

May/June

- Take any applicable AP exams.
- Your student should send their final transcript and student loan application(s) to their chosen college.
- Complete any remaining financial aid documents.
- Plan for college orientation, transportation, and housing.
- Your student should respond to all requests from colleges they are interested in attending.
- Graduation—your student is in the home stretch!
- Commit to a college they want to attend by May 1.

July

- Finalize college transportation and housing for the fall.
- Confirm housing and dining options at the school.
- Create a financial aid folder with the prior year's tax documents and begin collecting documentation for next year's FAFSA.
- Mark your calendar for October 1, when the FAFSA goes live.

THE BOTTOM LINE

- Encourage your student to start outlining essays and gathering the information necessary to fill out college applications the summer before senior year starts.
- Create a master calendar of dates and deadlines. Keep it updated—and in a place where everyone can see it.
- Help your student plan enough time to study for admissions tests. Take advantage of free tools on the SAT and ACT websites.
- Communicate with your student about concerns related to school, applications, and testing. This is a stressful time.

Get Your Money-Challenged Child Ready for College

THE ERICKSONS HAD WORKED WITH ME to get their daughter, Kristen, into the Ivy League school of her dreams, even though it was an enormous stretch for their family. It was going to mean a few lean years, but they were satisfied it was the right decision.

So, when Kristen's mother, Jamie, called me, distraught, I was very concerned that something had gone wrong. She explained that Kristen seemed unaware of how big a strain her choice was putting on the family budget. Kristen was excited but was talking about all the digital gadgets she would need for school, as well as the pricey dorm room decor she wanted from various catalogs. She was even texting her new roommate about where they would go for spring break.

Many high school students have absolutely no idea about how to manage their time or money. As a result, they turn into money-challenged, time-deprived college students. Money stress can be distracting, making it difficult to study, so it becomes a vicious cycle that creates even more stress. They take out student loans, open credit cards and max them out, spend foolishly, and often graduate late with a diploma and a big pile of debt.

One rule that I follow in working with families is that information is the number-one priority. If parents and students understand more about college and money, they make better decisions about college and money. As a parent, it is your responsibility to teach your children about money management. Not only will it make things easier on your family finances when your children head off to college, but they will also be better money managers when they graduate.

It's important to start teaching your child about money, budgeting, and saving early in life. Giving your child responsibility for saving toward big purchases, like a car, or teaching them how to budget their allowance helps them understand the value of their money and how hard they have to work for what they want. Such practices will also give them a head start when they get out in the world and have to manage their own money at college or after they get their first job. Of course, you want to give your child everything, but teaching them good financial skills will be a lifelong asset.

There are many theories about how allowance should be disbursed. Some people believe that allowance should be tied to chores while others think that undermines the concept that everyone needs to be contributing to the household without being paid to do so. Whatever you decide is right for your family, it's important to give your children responsibility for managing money early on so they understand that it is a finite resource—and when it's gone, it's gone. Start when they are little with appropriate amounts of money. Of course, you can still buy presents for birthdays and holidays, but make a point of saying that they will have to save some money and buy certain items for themselves. (And don't be tempted to cave in and buy it for them if they're struggling to save—the accomplishment and gratification is the point.) This teaches the value of money and establishes a cause-and-effect relationship in their mind.

AS THEY GET OLDER, SHARE MORE

Work with your child through the high school years to build a better understanding of the value of money, how to earn and use it, and what happens to those who rely on too much credit. When it comes time for a car, don't just purchase a brand-new vehicle. Sit down with your up-and-coming driver about a year or two before the planned purchase date. Explain how much a car costs, and talk about insurance, maintenance, and gasoline. Work out a budget that details how much money will be needed every year to keep the car running. And then set down the financial responsibilities. Talk about how much you are willing to invest as the parent, and let your child know they will be responsible for the rest. Then discuss ways of saving or earning money that can help achieve the goal.

The same process should be used in getting your child ready to attend college. Sometimes they are oblivious because you have not included them in the financial process. You say "yes" to a college you really can't afford because you don't want to disappoint your child, or you say "no" to a college without providing a reasonable explanation or offering alternatives. In addition to the "other talk," it's time to have the "money talk" with your money-challenged child.

WHAT TO SAY DURING THE MONEY TALK

The facts of money can be almost as daunting to explain as the facts of life, but equally necessary. Your student needs to understand where money comes from, what it takes to earn it, how it is spent, and what it means to be in debt.

Families differ in how open they are about money. Some share everything from annual income to debt load, while others speak in more general terms. I believe that more information is better, but your child also needs to understand that this is private information and not to be shared with others. You're trusting them with sensitive financial information to give a better understanding of the decisions your family can reasonably make. You may be taking on a substantial financial burden to allow your child the gift of attending college, so they will need to understand that the "Bank of Mom and Dad" may be closed during that period.

It's time to fully understand the financial impact college has on the student and the entire family. Here are some topics you will definitely need to cover.

What Attending College Will Cost

When discussing the cost of the college, some of the items you need to address include:

- A breakdown of tuition, room and board, fees, and other costs
- Cost of books and supplies
- Travel to and from school
- Expected spending money needed per week or month
- Any other expected out-of-pocket costs

Once you have shared a clear picture of all the costs related to college, also discuss how financial aid and scholarships will affect those decisions. Talk about student loan debt and its consequences—and how much you will need to take on to cover any differences. Many students are actually surprised at the amount of money their parents are investing in their future.

I know it's tough to have these conversations. We're taught that discussing money isn't polite. But your child is almost an adult, and you're investing an enormous amount of money in their future. This isn't the time to dance around a very serious issue for all of you.

The Budget

It is hard to meet expectations when you do not know what they are. How does a student know that they are spending too much money if there is no limit to what can be spent? Draw up a list of anticipated college expenses together, and then set out exactly how much you will be willing to cover as the parent. The rest will be up to your student. They will have the choice of cutting expenses or earning more money to make ends meet.

Ideally, this should be a lifelong conversation with your child, not a one-shot deal before they pack up the car to head off to college. You have to be persistent, especially throughout the high school years. You are providing a financial education to someone who will receive a lifetime of benefit and is in need of all the financial management skills you have been teaching.

There's an App for That

Haul out a pencil and paper, and your student is probably going to roll their eyes. Today, most young people do everything on their phones or other devices through apps. That's good news because there are some great apps to help your student manage their money:

- **Mint**: Connects to your student's bank accounts, credit cards, investments, and other financial accounts, showing them in one dashboard interface so they can create a budget, track spending, receive bill reminders, and get tips from the app about saving money, budgeting, and reducing fees.

- **LearnVest**: LearnVest lets your student track their budget and set goals. The app even has planners who can give advice about achieving long-term spending goals. LearnVest has plenty of content to help your student learn to save money, budget better, manage debt, and invest for the long term.

Most of these types of apps are free for the basic version, with premium versions available that have more features. (This is called a "freemium" model.) These are two highly rated apps, but you should investigate the many options that are out there and find the one that best meets your student's needs.

The Extras

Once on campus, the sense of freedom is palpable and the mix of students is exciting. Students may immediately start making plans for joining fraternities and sororities, ski weekends, and spring break in the Caribbean. It can be disappointing for both your child and you to have to forgo these fun extras if they're not in the budget. However, it's critical to keep focused on the goal: Graduate from college with as little debt as possible. Missing out on spring break is a small price to pay for greater long-term financial security.

The Challenges of Graduating in Four Years

Most families' budgets include four years to pay for a child's bachelor's degree. However, many don't understand that the majority of students don't complete their degrees in four years. Think about what it would do to your budget to have to suddenly field an extra year of school—or even two. According to the U.S. Department of Education, the median time it took students to earn their bachelor's degree is 52 months—roughly a full extra semester. In the latest numbers available, just 44 percent of students achieved their degrees in a four-year time frame.[5]

Among the reasons for this disparity are the need for remedial classes among some students. If your child needs remedial math or language arts classes, those will eat up credits and time that were budgeted for earning their degree. Sometimes, courses needed for a certain major aren't offered when needed or students change majors, which requires additional coursework. There are also cases where students simply don't keep up with the 15-credit load per semester that they need to achieve the typical 120-credit graduation requirement.

Your student's adviser can be invaluable in helping them stay on track. While it may be tempting to take a ceramics or wine-tasting class, it's critical to use the four-year time period wisely to ensure they are taking the appropriate classes to graduate with their intended major. Taking Advanced Placement (AP) courses in high school or core curriculum classes at a local community college during the summer months can help get you back on track with much less expense than paying for an additional semester or more of tuition, room and board, fees, and other expenses. Be sure your student is aware of the challenges to graduating within the four years for which you have budgeted.

Their Role in Paying for College

Many parents fail to explain exactly what they expect from their college student in terms of financial responsibility. They take care of all the financial aid forms, fill out the student loan applications, pay the tuition bills, and never let their child worry about a thing. At graduation, they congratulate their darling child, and then drop the bombshell of how much money is due on student loans. The graduate is shocked—shocked—to find out how much money is owed and realizes it is going to be a very difficult start to life.

This is not ideal or even fair. Students need to understand the debt for which they are becoming responsible. After all, even if parents plan on paying the loans, the student is ultimately responsible for paying them and the loans affect their credit. Discuss the accumulating debt, what monthly payments are estimated to be, and help your student understand this obligation.

The Quest for Money

Let your child know that the more money you can pay as a family, the less you will have to borrow as a family. Keep scouring the Internet for any and all scholarships. Spell out whether your child will be expected to participate in a work-study program or hold a part-time job, and how much money needs to be earned over the summer to cover out-of-pocket expenses. "Job" is not a dirty word—it's a reality. If your child understands how challenging it is to balance earning and learning, they're more likely to spend thoughtfully.

The New Frugality

Use every means at your disposal to cut costs whenever possible. Instead of having a car on campus or taking an airplane or train home, share rides if there is travel involved in getting to the college campus. Find out how to buy used or digital books to save money. Evaluate the costs of a meal plan vs. buying food and cooking. Every penny that is saved is one that will not have to be borrowed.

Teach Your Child about Credit

In the past generation, we have become accustomed to easy credit. Credit card applications come spilling out of the mailbox, mortgage approvals come easy, and refinanced loans are readily available. Then, something happens like a medical emergency or job loss, and the whole house of cards comes tumbling down.

Children who have observed the use of easy credit all their lives begin to believe that nothing should be out of reach. They get credit cards and cars while they are in high school and have no idea where the money comes from to pay for these things. Parents need to be very clear in explaining how quickly interest builds, especially on credit cards, and what happens when you can only make minimum payments. Even if nothing else is purchased using a card, it can still take years and years to pay it off because of the interest that has accrued.

THE NEW GENERATION

It is most probable that students who will be benefiting from this information and advice belong to the millennial generation. This generation has a whole new take on everything from money and jobs to computers and education. While the baby boomers were content to take on the values and work ethics of their heavily immigrant parents, the millennials are setting a new standard for themselves and blazing new trails in everything they do.

An astonishing change in mindset is about to take place in American culture as the impact of the baby boomer generation fades and the millennials finally become the dominant force in society. Depending on their age, some have already faced a massive recession, learned about the dangers of easy credit, and are learning to cope with a new financial reality. As the generation that will have the most economic impact in the next 20 to 30 years, it's smart to start learning about money management now.

But the younger millennials are just beginning their journey. The lessons their parents are imparting to them now are going to shape the economic future of our country for many years to come. It is the parent's responsibility to teach these lessons well so you won't have to worry about why your college freshman can't handle money better.

THE BOTTOM LINE

- Explain that this advice is for your child's long-term security. You trust your student and want them to understand the financial decisions that are being made.
- Invite him or her to come up with ideas to help save money or earn more toward college.
- Be honest. There's no sense in pretending that the sky's the limit when it comes to affording college, if it isn't. It's also not fair to obligate a child to student loan debt without them fully understanding the long-term ramifications.

PART 2

PAYING THE WAY

How Does All This Work, Anyway?

FRANCINE IS A SINGLE MOM WITH TWINS who are seniors in high school. She has been too terrified to begin looking seriously at her assets or the financial aid process. As a result, when it was time to begin filling out the FAFSA form, she realized that assets her parents had gifted to her children to help pay for college should have been put in a 529 account, where they would be counted less. In addition, she had taken advantage of an uptick in the market to sell off some stocks at an impressive gain, which also decreased her financial aid amount. Because she waited too long to begin the process and hadn't sought the advice of a financial planner before she made these decisions, she took a hit on the amount of financial aid for which she qualified.

So many people are confused about the financial aid process. And it is somewhat tricky to understand. You fill out a form and hand over all your financial data. Then, it goes through some mysterious electronic portal, and you get an estimate of what the Powers That Be think you can pay toward your child's college education, which is called your Expected Family Contribution, or EFC. Schools may offer you various combinations of money—some more than others—to help you make up the difference. And you're left wondering what the heck just happened. It's a bit more straightforward than that Wizard-of-Oz description. The federal government has its own formula to calculate your EFC. Information about this can be found at StudentAid.gov under the "Who Gets Aid" tab. In addition, colleges, universities, community colleges, trade schools, and other post-secondary education institutions may have their own calculations they apply to determine how much aid they'll award, which may be a different amount from the EFC.

Ultimately, the financial aid staff at the college or university determines the amount of aid you will receive. First, the staff compares the cost of attendance (COA) to your EFC as determined by the FAFSA you filed. Remember, your COA is the total amount to attend the school, including tuition, room and board, books, fees, transportation, and other expenses. The difference between the two is your financial need.

HOW DO THEY DECIDE WHO GETS WHAT?

I like to explain the process colleges use for determining financial aid as "buckets of money." The college has some, like the merit aid the admissions office awards for academic, athletic, music, or other excellence. The federal government dictates some, such as the amount of Pell Grants or student loans for which the student might qualify. The financial aid office determines resources like scholarships, grants, the Federal Work-Study (FWS) Program, loans, and other possible resources. In addition, some money may be available from third-party sources, like scholarships, grants, and other programs.

While "financial aid" is typically viewed as one big pot of money, it's important to understand the different types of aid and how each is awarded. Colleges award both merit aid and financial aid, which are different. Financial aid includes scholarships, grants, loans, and work-study programs that are government-sponsored or may be offered by the school itself and is typically need-based or non-need-based. Merit aid is offered by the school. Aid that does not come from the federal or state government may come from the institution itself in the form of grants or scholarships, and you will see it listed in the financial aid award letter or acceptance letter you receive from each college. Here's what you need to know about each:

- **Need-based:** This is financial aid that is awarded based on your family's ability to pay for your student's college education. It is determined from the information provided on the FAFSA and your EFC, but you cannot receive more need-based aid than the amount the school has estimated for your financial need. Don't assume you make too much money, as there are other factors that may be taken into consideration, such as the parents' age or number of students in college. Need-based awards may include grants, subsidized student loans, and work-study programs. Note that some of this aid may come in the form of federal student loans that will have to be repaid. Be sure to complete the financial aid application as early as possible, as some need-based awards are given on a first-come, first-served basis.

- **Non-need-based:** Students may also receive aid that is not related to their financial need. When awarding non-need-based aid, colleges look at the COA, then subtract the amount of aid your child has received, such as merit aid, need-based financial aid, private scholarships, and other sources. The balance may be met with non-need-based financial aid, which may include loan programs like the federal PLUS Loan, Direct Unsubsidized Loans, and others.

- **Merit-based:** This type of aid is usually awarded after your student has been admitted to the college and is typically based on your child's achievements. Those achievements may be academic, artistic, or athletic, and often vary widely from school to school. So, if your child is a gifted pianist or the top-rated soccer player in your state and wants to continue playing in college, they may be awarded scholarships or other forms of aid to do so. This award is often made before or in conjunction with the college's financial aid award. Most of these do not have a financial component, so a student with a wealthy background is just as entitled to a merit-based award as a student with more limited financial means.

- **Situational:** Colleges may have scholarships and endowments available that are awarded to students for various reasons. These may be based on ethnic background, medical condition, financial circumstances, course of study, or other factors set out by the sponsor. You can never be certain what scholarships are available at each individual school until your child applies, and you find out what has been awarded.

GETTING THE MONEY

So with all those buckets of money, how do you get some to flow your way? Early in the fall of your child's senior year, or the summer before if possible, take a look at the application requirements for your child's selected schools. If the school requires a CSS Profile, or if your child is thinking about seeking early admission, you may need to make some financial moves before the end of the year. With the new FAFSA, you may begin filling out the form as early as October of your child's senior year. The purpose of completing either the FAFSA or the CSS Profile is to try to determine how much money your family can contribute to the cost of your child's education. It helps colleges determine how much financial aid they are going to offer to your child.

Both financial aid application forms will ask for the previous year's federal income tax amounts. They are also looking for information on taxed and untaxed income and

Need-based vs. Non-need-based Financial Aid

Using arbitrary numbers, the calculation for need-based and non-need-based aid might look like this:

Need-based Aid

COA:	$25,438
Less EFC:	$14,766
Financial Need:	$10,672

That means you are only eligible to receive up to $10,672 in need-based federal student aid. Those programs include:

- Federal Pell Grants
- Federal Supplemental Educational Opportunity Grants
- Direct Subsidized Loans
- Federal Work-Study (FWS) employment

But that's not all there is. There are also resources for non-need-based aid. The school will take the COA and subtract the amount of aid you were awarded, taking into consideration all sources, including private scholarships. Taking the previous example, and assuming the school awarded $5,000 in merit aid, your non-need eligibility would look like this:

Non-need-based Aid

COA:	$25,438
Less EFC:	$14,766
Merit Aid:	$5,000
Non-need-based Aid:	$5,672

This formula is a calculation of the COA less the amount of merit aid awarded. Federal non-need-based resources include:

- Direct Unsubsidized Loans
- Direct PLUS Loans
- Teacher Education Access for College and Higher Education (TEACH) grants

benefits, as well as information on savings accounts, 529 savings accounts, stock holdings, and other investments. It can definitely pay to be strategic when it comes to planning for financial aid. However, for a variety of reasons, it's a bad idea to try to "game" the system to get more aid. First, you're submitting information to the federal government, and there are consequences for not being truthful. In addition, you need to submit this form every year. If your financial situation changes drastically, so will your financial aid package. Here are some common moves people think about making and their potential impact, for better or worse. However, before you make any financial moves, it's important to understand their impact on your personal financial situation, so it's a good idea to consult with your tax adviser or financial planner.

- **529 plans:** There is a great deal of misunderstanding when it comes to 529 plans. Contributions are not tax-deductible, but the earnings grow free from federal tax. They may also offer some state tax benefits, but that varies from state to state and may depend on the program in which you invest. (Each state has its own 529 plan options, but you're not limited to investing in those offered by your state.) If you have a 529 savings plan, it is important to know who is considered the owner. Sometimes grandparents try to help out by establishing a 529 plan, only to find that it may affect their grandchild's ability to receive financial aid. Some people even hesitate to begin saving for their children in a 529 plan because they're afraid that it will reduce the amount of aid to which they're entitled.

However, 529 plans are treated differently depending on who owns them. If it is a parental asset—a plan started by a parent for the benefit of the child—it is reported as such on the FAFSA. Any qualified distributions from this type of account are not treated as income. While third-party owners, such as grandparents, do not have to report the plans on the FAFSA, the distributions from them can be considered untaxed income for their grandchild.

GOOD TO KNOW

529 Plans and Financial Aid

Financial aid calculations don't count the entire balance of the 529 plan. For accounts owned by the parents, approximately 5.64 percent of the balance is counted toward financial aid calculations. If the account is owned by grandparents or other third parties, the distributions to the student are counted as income and can have a much greater impact on financial aid calculations. Some financial planners may recommend keeping a grandparent-opened 529 plan in the grandparents' name until after the FAFSA is filed, and then transferring the plan to the parents' name before any distributions are made.

- **Retirement accounts:** Some parents do not want it to appear that they have an ample amount of cash on hand, so they decide to make the legally allowed contribution to a tax-advantaged retirement account, such as a 401(k) or individual retirement account

(IRA). You may decrease your income and taxes due, but that could also be problematic if you suddenly need cash. Taking money out of a tax-advantaged retirement account may result in a penalty on your federal income taxes.

- **Home improvements:** Using available cash to invest in capital improvements for your home may have certain tax advantages. Home improvements may help you enjoy your home more and may even result in higher resale value. The risk is that an increased home value may also increase your local property taxes and will decrease the available cash on hand in case of emergencies. In addition, schools that use the CSS Profile consider home equity, so an increase in home value and other factors could have an impact on the following year's financial aid calculations.
- **Mortgages:** Some families think there might be a benefit to selling their investment portfolios to pay off a mortgage on the family's home, so it won't look like they have a large amount of money available. A financial planner can provide a rough estimate of how much your portfolio is worth based on current market conditions, and will help you determine how much of a gain or loss you will have to absorb with the sale. This sale could also have tax implications, depending on whether you are incurring short- or long-term gains and losses.
- **Inheritances:** If you have any control over assets that are to be sold as part of an inheritance, try to do it in years prior to those you will be reporting on the

financial aid forms. If you cannot control the timing, you may wish to consider whether it makes sense to gift any part of the inheritance to family members other than the student or to make a contribution to the student's 529 plan.

Keep in mind that you and your student will be filling out these financial aid forms for the entire time your child is in school. While you may succeed in securing a large amount of financial aid for your child's freshman year in college, you will need to show similar income for the sophomore year. If your taxable income or liquid assets increase greatly over the next four or five years, you may be paying a much higher tuition in your child's remaining years of college.

This discussion is not meant to be taken as any type of definite recommendation. Each family situation is different, and no one solution is best for every family. If you are thinking of taking any of these moves, it is best to consult the appropriate tax and financial planner as well as your financial aid officer before making any of these moves. You want to know how the choices you make now affect not only your child, but also your family. You need time to consult any necessary adviser to make those decisions as well as to take action if you need to do so.

It is a good idea to familiarize yourself with the forms earlier in the year, as there are any number of other variables. Student's dependency status, parents' divorce, unmarried parents, step-parents, widowed parents, incarcerated parents, or uncooperative parents can all impact your financial aid application form. If it's October of your child's senior year and you're just figuring this out, it's already too late to do anything about it, and the financial aid will be based on the current information you provide.

On the other hand, it is entirely possible that your family situation won't require any type of thought process similar to this. Your income may be low enough that you will automatically qualify for need-based scholarships, you could have sufficient funds already saved, or your child might qualify for an academic or athletic scholarship. Still, it is always best to think ahead in case there are things you can do now to make sure you are able to maximize the amount of financial aid your child receives.

THE BOTTOM LINE

- Begin looking at the FAFSA and your finances early to familiarize yourself with the assets counted, as well as to begin thinking about appropriate financial moves.
- Understand the differences between need-based, merit-based, and non-need-based aid—there are many options to pay for college.
- Don't be afraid of 529 plans! They are great savings vehicles for your child's college education.
- Before making big financial moves, always seek the advice of a qualified tax accountant, financial planner, or financial aid consultant.

Taking the Fear Out of the FAFSA

ANTHONY MAGLONE HAD SAVED MONEY in a Uniform Gifts to Minors Act (UGMA) account for his daughter, Rita, since her birth. Now, she's a junior in high school. Not only did he manage to put away $11,500 for her education, but Rita also has three savings bonds valued at $2,200. He called me after a friend told him that those would count negatively toward Rita's financial aid calculations, since they were in her name. Anthony was worried and disheartened that his saving might have actually hurt her chances to go to college.

He needed advice on whether he should or could change the type of account the money was in—such as moving it to a 529 savings plan, which might count less when calculating their EFC. He also wanted to know when to start using the funds. Was it best for them to use all the money for Rita's freshman year of college, which would leave them with no assets to show on the following year's FAFSA? Or should they allocate a portion for each year and borrow the rest?

Families often experience angst, concern, and confusion when confronting the college financial aid application. They tear their collective hair out trying to decide which approach is best, argue with ex-partners, and throw their hands up in surrender. It can seem overwhelming. And, since every situation is unique, there's no universal answer.

However, that's not to say there isn't an answer for *your* family. Of course there is. It lies in the Free Application for Federal Student Aid, commonly known as the FAFSA, which is possibly one of the most feared terms among adults with college-age children. Never has something with the word "free" in its title caused so much anguish!

The FAFSA is an online form that is the gateway to federal and state financial aid options, including federal student loans, Pell Grants, and federal work-study program participation, to name a few. Colleges and universities may also use it to determine their own financial aid awards. Depending on the school your child chooses, you may also need to fill out a CSS Profile, another assessment tool used in awarding institutional aid.

College financial aid officers use information from the application, including income and assets, to get an accurate picture of the family's financial situation. Then, using federal guidelines for federal aid options, as well as their own internal guidelines for other awards, they determine how much the family can afford and how much assistance will be required in financial aid to enable the child to attend their school.

In 2015, the Federal Student Aid office of the Department of Education announced some important changes to the FAFSA and its deadlines. Beginning with the 2017-2018 school year, whether your child is just starting college or a continuing student, families submit their FAFSA forms in October instead of January. Parents of students going to college in 2017 are able to file their financial aid forms in October 2016 using their 2015 financial data. Here's what the change looks like for future and continuing students:

College Year	FAFSA Submission Window	Using Tax Information From
July 1, 2015 to June 30, 2016	January 1, 2015 to June 30, 2016	2014
July 1, 2016 to June 30, 2017	January 1, 2016 to June 30, 2017	2015
July 1, 2017 to June 30, 2018	October 1, 2016 to June 30, 2017	2015
July 1, 2018 to June 30, 2019	October 1, 2017 to June 30, 2019	2016

Source: Federal Student Aid, U.S. Department of Education

Why the change? The Department of Education believes it will benefit the students. The revised timeline follows the college admissions process more closely, and parents can use real data from the previous year to fill out the form instead of estimating—perhaps wrongly—items like total income and taxes paid. It also allows parents more time to explore their financial aid options and be sure they're filing the FAFSA before state deadlines, which may be different from federal deadlines.

WAIT, WHO COMPLETES THE FAFSA?

Ah, this is the big question. We've been talking about having your student take responsibility for much of the college application process, like getting the applications completed and writing essays. The FAFSA is considered a student form. But when it comes to filling out the FAFSA, students must report their parents' income and assets—information that might not be readily available to them. So, it's a good idea to fill it out together.

Who Counts as a "Parent"?

The FAFSA has specific guidelines about who will provide information. A legal parent is a biological or adoptive parent, or a parent as determined by the state—for example, if the parent is listed on the student's birth certificate. If the student has a step-parent, you generally also must provide information about them. In addition:

- If the student's parents are married, information about both must be included.
- If the student's parents are not married to each other but live together, both parents' financial information must be included. This holds true even if the parents were never married or if they are divorced or separated, but still live together.
- If the parents are not married and do not live with each other, use the information for the

parent with whom the child lives most of the time. If that parent has remarried, the student will also need to include financial information for the step-parent.

What about Other Circumstances?

Even if the student does not live with their parent or parents, that information must still be reported. Grandparents, foster parents, legal guardians, older siblings, uncles or aunts, and widowed step-parents are not considered parents unless the student has been legally adopted by them.

If student is dependent and unable to provide information about their parents for some reason, they have the option to indicate that they have special circumstances that leave them unable to obtain their parents' information. The online FAFSA site will then allow them to submit their application without entering data about their parents. However, it will not be fully processed. They will not receive an Expected Family Contribution (EFC) and must immediately contact the financial aid office at the school they plan to attend. They may be asked to provide additional documentation regarding their situation. Also, note that a parent's citizenship does not affect a student's ability to receive federal financial aid. If parents do not have a Social Security numbers (SSN), all zeroes should be entered in that field.

If a student's parents do not support them in their efforts to attend college or refuse to supply financial information, they can select the option that states they cannot provide information and there are special circumstances involved.

They can still submit their FAFSA without their information, but they will not be able to receive any federal student aid other than an unsubsidized loan, and even that might not happen if they cannot show some type of ability to repay it. If this is the case, they must also contact the financial aid office at the school they plan to attend.

FILLING OUT THE FAFSA

The FAFSA is completed online at https://fafsa.ed.gov. I'm not going to sugarcoat it: I can honestly say that I have never met anybody who enjoyed the process. Perhaps they were happy with the outcome once the financial aid award letters started to arrive, but it can be an arduous process.

However, I believe that every parent of a college-age student should fill out the form. Virtually every student may be entitled to some form of financial aid. And if you don't fill out the form, you may not be eligible for the aid available to your family. So, let's dive in and discuss the process.

Get Your Documents Ready

So, you and your student have finally gotten yourselves geared up to complete the FAFSA. You're at the computer, making progress and all of a sudden you realize you're missing necessary information. Two hours later, after you have turned the whole house upside down, you just don't have the energy to tackle it again. Your momentum is lost, and the process drags on.

Avoid such delays and frustration by gathering your documentation well before you sit down to fill out the form. If you are planning on submitting your application in October, take some time during the summer to prepare. Keep a big file—either on paper or on a computer—with copies of the information you need.

FAFSA Documentation Checklist

Filling out the FAFSA requires piecing together a comprehensive picture of your family's income and assets. Use this checklist to ensure you have everything you need before you start.

☐ Social Security number for the student and parents, if the student is a dependent child

☐ Driver's license number, if the student has one

☐ Alien Registration Number, if the student is not a U.S. citizen

☐ Federal tax information (or foreign tax return) or tax returns, including W-2 or 1099 information, for the student and for the parents of a dependent student

☐ Records of untaxed income, such as self-employment income, child support, interest earned, and veterans' noneducation benefits for the student and for the parents of a dependent student

☐ Information on cash, savings, and checking account balances

☐ Investment information, including stocks and bonds and real estate, but not including the home in which you live

☐ Business and farm assets for the student and for the parents of a dependent student

Get a Federal Student Aid ID

The U.S. Department of Education administers a Federal Student Aid User ID system, which is similar to the user-name/email and password prompts used on most websites. The FSA ID will be used to confirm your identity when accessing several U.S. Department of Education websites.

Your FSA ID has the same legal status as your written signature and can be used to electronically sign legally binding documents online. Safeguard this information as you do all of your usernames and passwords, so it doesn't fall into the wrong hands. Parents and students can apply for their FSA ID at any time at fsaid.ed.gov.

Take Your Time, But Don't Miss the Deadline

Filling out the FAFSA is not some sort of timed exercise. Take your time, think about the questions, and provide accurate information. On the other hand, though, you don't want to draw the process out too long. While you technically have until June 30 to complete the FAFSA, you must pay very close attention to the school's financial aid deadline and your state's financial aid deadline. Be sure to check the deadlines, as some schools are earlier than others.

Get Help If Needed

While the Department of Education wants to have a good understanding of your financial situation, they really do try to make the form as easy as possible to complete. They also provide a number of free resources to help find answers to your questions. Check out the help section of the FAFSA website at https://fafsa.ed.gov/help.htm.

Allow for Processing Time

Depending on volume, it can take anywhere from one to four weeks to process your FAFSA. If you left out information or made a mistake, it will take even more time before colleges can upload your FAFSA data into their systems. Many students miss out on financial aid simply by waiting until the last minute to complete the FAFSA and then find out they have no time if errors or other unforeseen circumstances occur.

Check for Your Mistakes

By far, the leading cause of students not receiving the maximum amount of financial aid to which they are entitled is mistakes that are made when completing the FAFSA. The most common mistake is an unlikely one: the student's name. Never use a nickname or abbreviated name—the name and Social Security number on the FAFSA must match what is on the student's Social Security card. Make sure your home and email addresses are correct so you will receive your Student Aid Report via email. Try not to leave any fields blank. Answer "zero" or "not applicable," if necessary. Also, the FAFSA must be signed with the student's and parent's FSA ID to be processed, but you can submit without signatures. Any of these oversights could result in processing delays or reduced financial aid. The top mistake that leads to less aid, as opposed to delays in the receipt of aid, is counting retirement plan accounts and home equity as investments.

Look for Their Mistakes

Once your information is complete and your form is processed, your student will receive a Student Aid Report that lists an EFC. The EFC will also be listed on the confirmation page. This will also be provided to your student's selected colleges. Be sure to review this information carefully, as mistakes can dramatically affect the amount of financial aid your student receives. Contact Federal Student

Aid or visit their website to learn how you can correct any errors, and also alert the schools to which your student has applied.

Know What You Can Change

There are certain things that can and cannot be changed on the FAFSA and certain things that must be changed if your circumstances change. Your application may also be selected for a process called verification, in which you will be asked to provide additional documentation to substantiate certain elements of the application. This does not mean there is a problem; it is simply a request for clarification. Try to provide the necessary information as soon as possible.

The online FAFSA does not allow you to change your Social Security number. If it is wrong, ask the financial aid office at the school your student plans to attend whether they should start over and submit a new FAFSA. You may update your mailing address, email address, and other contact information, and you can add additional schools. Always update anything that changes the student's dependency status. If selected for verification, some questions will include whether there has been a change in the number of family members in the parents' or student's household, or if there has been a change in the number of people in the parents' household who are in college.

Once your FAFSA is submitted, it is possible that your family might experience some type of event that dramatically affects your financial situation. This might include a medical emergency, natural disaster, or job loss. While your FAFSA information must be current as of the date it is submitted, your student should contact the designated schools and explain your particular situation. Be prepared to provide documentation.

Verification? What's That?

You and your student have filled out the FAFSA. Now you can sit back and wait for your student's aid package to come in. While you are waiting, you may get a notification that the college needs more documentation to verify what you've submitted.

Take a deep breath and stay calm. Verification is something we rarely hear about when it comes to financial aid applications, but it happens often. The Department of Education requires the college to verify certain application elements. So, they may ask for additional proof of income or household size, for example. It's not anything to worry about, especially if you were careful in filling out your FAFSA. But respond with the additional documentation as soon as you can so you don't lose out on financial aid due to a delay.

GETTING THE MOST AID

While there are certainly some smart financial moves you can make to maximize the amount of financial aid your child receives, keep in mind that you will have to keep this up for at least four years, and more if you have more than one child attending college. Moves you make to maximize financial aid this year could increase your taxes or affect next year's aid eligibility. The best strategy is to present an accurate, consistent picture of your financial situation so the college can make a reasonable judgment about how much aid they will grant. Remember that I'm not a financial or tax adviser, and you should always consult such professionals when making big financial moves to determine the impact they'll have on your personal financial situation.

Typically, it's a good idea to not have too much money in the student's name, as it is assessed at a higher rate when calculating your EFC. It might make sense to draw down some liquid assets and try to pay off bills such as credit card debt or your mortgage, since home equity is typically not used on the FAFSA as part of your aid calculation.

Keep in mind, though, that any moves should be made well before you complete the FAFSA, and there could be other repercussions in terms of penalties or taxes due. Since you will also have to file a FAFSA for four years or more, you will need to reflect the same financial situation throughout your child's college career to maintain the same level of aid. Discuss the positives and negatives with a professional financial adviser before making any definite moves.

MYTHBUSTERS: THE FAFSA EDITION

Myths swirl around the FAFSA. Parents talk to one another, read posts on social media, or make assumptions based on rumors they have heard. Let's set the record straight and debunk some of these myths so you can make smart choices when it comes to paying for your child's college education.

- **I have to pay to submit the FAFSA.** Although The College Board collects a fee to process the CSS Profile, the Free Application for Federal Student Aid is just that—free. There are online imposters that may try to lure you in with promises of scholarships or guarantees of financial aid, so be sure you only use the official government site at www.fafsa.ed.gov.

- **I need to estimate next year's taxes.** Now that the FAFSA is completed with the previous year's financial information, you don't need to estimate. Fortunately, the handy IRS Data Retrieval Tool, which can be accessed from the FAFSA application, makes this process much simpler.
- **We don't make enough money to afford college.** Never make that assumption, because this is exactly what this form is trying to determine. Colleges have access to many different types of financial aid. If they are interested in your student, and understand your financial picture completely, they may be able to put together a very competitive financial aid offer. There is no income minimum. In some cases, I have found that it would actually cost the parents less to send their student to a private college with a good financial aid package than it would to enroll in a public university that cannot offer substantial financial aid.
- **We make too much money to qualify for financial aid.** This can be a costly assumption as there are many different types of financial aid. There are federal, state, and institutional aid opportunities, and even some scholarships that rely on FAFSA information. Some aid is indeed income-based, but there is also merit-based aid, and you will never know if your child qualifies if you don't apply. Factors such as the parents' age or the size of your family also

factor into the equation, so how do you know for sure that you earn too much? Some colleges review the entire picture of academic and athletic achievements, extracurricular activities, and financial circumstances to determine their level of interest in each student.

- **My child's grades aren't good enough.** That may have more of an impact on the application process than the financial aid process. While some aid is merit-based, your child may still be eligible for other types of aid. File the FAFSA, and let the college decide. If granted admission, your child will have to meet certain minimum academic requirements to continue qualifying for financial aid.

- **We're just going to borrow the money.** You should never borrow more than you need, but even if this is your strategy, you should still file the FAFSA. You may qualify for subsidized or unsubsidized federal student loans. These have low interest rates and could save you money in the long term.

- **I'm not eligible for federal aid.** There are some cases when students are not eligible for federal student aid, but that doesn't mean there is no state or institutional aid available. Whether or not you think you're eligible, you should complete the FAFSA to be sure. Typically, eligibility for federal financial aid requires that your student:

  o Is a U.S. citizen or eligible noncitizen
  o Has a valid Social Security number

- ○ Is registered with the Selective Service if a male (who must enroll between the ages of 18 and 25)
- ○ Be enrolled or accepted for enrollment as a regular student in an eligible degree or certificate program
- ○ Is not currently in default on a student loan and plans to use the loan for education purposes
- ○ Has a high school diploma or equivalent

There are other basic criteria, which you can find at https://studentaid.ed.gov/sa/eligibility/basic-criteria. In addition, being convicted of certain crimes can limit a student's eligibility.

- **Our circumstances are unique.** Some family situations can be highly unusual due to medical emergencies, natural disasters, or dire financial circumstances. In these cases, it is best to talk directly to the school's financial aid office to determine the best strategy. Some colleges have special programs available that are designed to help students in dire financial need. Be prepared to provide documentation for any claims you make.
- **We have plenty of time.** This is perhaps the most dangerous myth of all. The FAFSA application is online beginning in October, but many parents think they have until the end of June to complete it. While this may be technically true, it is best to get the application completed and submitted as early as possible. There are certain forms of financial aid

that are limited, so they are only available on a first-come, first-served basis. You could severely limit your chances of maximizing financial aid simply by waiting too long.

Perhaps the most self-defeating statement regarding the FAFSA is "It's just too hard, so we're not going to bother." Even if they attempt to complete the form, some parents don't put their best effort into it. The only people they are hurting are themselves and their student. There are many ways to obtain help, but you might have to ask for it first.

THE BOTTOM LINE

- The FAFSA timeline has changed. Know the new deadline dates.
- It's almost always a good idea to fill out the FAFSA—most students are eligible for some sort of aid.
- Be prepared. Use our checklist to line up your documents before you fill out the form so you have all of the information you need.
- Submit early. Some financial aid is awarded on a rolling basis, so early submissions have a better shot at landing more financial aid.
- Check and double-check the form for errors, and respond to any requests for verification promptly.
- Don't believe the myths. Every circumstance is unique. Fill out the form and get what your family is entitled to.

7

Understanding Different Types of Aid

GABRIEL AND SOFIA MORENO WERE WORRIED about how they were going to manage college costs for their two sons. David, a junior, was an average student with a 2.9 GPA. He wasn't an athlete, but he was involved in Advancement Via Individual Determination, or AVID, which helps support students from underrepresented groups. A friend told them about a scholarship opportunity for Latino students who would be the first generation to go to college, but they were afraid that David's grades would make him ineligible.

With roughly $60,000 in annual income, the Morenos were going to need every dime they could find to afford college for David and their younger son, Jimmy, who was a freshman. If David received the AVID scholarship, it was still likely that they could only afford to send Jimmy to community college for two years if he didn't qualify for the same scholarship. Once Jimmy finished his associate's degree at the community college, they would determine if they could afford to send him for his bachelor's degree, but it bothered them that they could not afford to offer the same opportunity to both sons. The Morenos had decisions to make on many fronts—some were related to financial aid, some to scholarships, and others to cost comparisons.

It's difficult to speculate about the amount of financial aid a family will receive because so many factors affect the award, ranging from household size, family income, number of family members in college, age of the oldest parent, and others. You can get an idea by using the FAFSA4caster found at https://studentaid.ed.gov/sa/fafsa/estimate. (For more information and to find another estimator, see the "Good to Know: Estimating Tools" box on page 106.)

However, for financial aid decision-makers to truly assess your situation, it's important to fill out the full FAFSA—and the CSS Profile, if your child's preferred college requires it. You don't know what is available at any given college until your student completes an admissions application and requests financial aid. That's when your family can really start making decisions based on facts.

Be sure to read the financial aid award letters carefully so you know how much is considered "free" money, how much must be worked for, and how much will need to be repaid. While you do not have to take the student loans that are offered, you'll have to find other ways to pay for the difference. That might include some combination of savings, gifts, scholarships, grants, or work-study programs.

FINANCIAL AID OPTIONS—THERE MAY BE MORE THAN YOU THINK!

The actual monetary aid for post-secondary schooling comes in many different forms. So, when we talk about "financial aid," it's not all one thing. The various forms typically fall into four key categories:

- Grants
- Scholarships
- Work-study programs
- Loans

The sources of these forms of aid are typically the federal or state government; college, university, or other post-secondary school your student is attending; or private organizations.

FIRST, THE FEDERAL AID

When it comes to education in this country, the federal government is one of the biggest sources of aid, mostly in the forms of grants and student loans, both subsidized and unsubsidized. There are a number of types of student loans, which we'll discuss in Chapter 8.

Grants

The federal government offers several different types of grants to students attending college or post-secondary schools. Grants are coveted forms of aid because they don't have to be repaid. They simply offset your child's COA (cost of attendance, remember?). Some of the types of grants offered by the federal government include:

GOOD TO KNOW

Estimating Tools

Most need-based grants, scholarships, loans, and other forms of financial aid have financial thresholds for eligibility. However, it's almost never as simple as "If my family makes X dollars per year, then my child is eligible." Plus, these amounts change nearly every year. As a result, I made a decision not to include such thresholds because they are misleading. Instead, a better way to estimate your financial aid award is to use the FAFSA4caster, which will give you a rough idea of the aid for which your family will qualify.

Another useful tool is the College Board's Net Price Calculator (http://netpricecalculator.collegeboard.org/), which can help you estimate the "net price" to attend a particular college or university. Your net price is the "full cost"—which includes tuition, room and board, books, supplies, fees, transportation, and personal expenses—less any grants and scholarships for which your student might be eligible.

Federal Pell Grants

These grants are typically awarded to undergraduate students who have not yet earned a bachelor's degree, but some teacher certification programs might meet eligibility criteria, too. Your child's eligibility is determined by financial need. Each year, the grant has a maximum—in the 2015-2016 school year, it was $5,775, for example, although some students who had a parent who died serving in Iraq or Afghanistan may be eligible for higher amounts. Students cannot receive Pell Grants for more than six years. Every student who meets the requirements can get a Pell Grant if they apply.

Federal Supplemental Educational Opportunity Grants (FSEOG)
This type of grant may be an option if students qualify based on financial need and if their chosen school participates in the program, so check with the financial aid office to find out. These grants typically total between $100 and $4,000 per year. This is first-come, first-served aid, as schools receive a limited amount of these funds. The financial aid director awards these grants, which are typically only awarded to students who also receive Pell Grants.

Teacher Education Assistance for College and Higher Education (TEACH) Grants
TEACH Grants are awarded up to $4,000 per year to students who are studying to become teachers. Government budget cuts may affect the amount your student receives. According to the Federal Student Aid website the recipient must sign a grant agreement in which they agree to teach:

- In a high-need field
- In an elementary school, secondary school, or educational service agency that serves students from low-income families
- For at least four complete academic years within eight years of completing or ceasing enrollment in the course of study for which they received the grant.

If the grant recipient does not complete their service obligation, the grant funds received are converted into a Direct Unsubsidized Loan that must be repaid to the U.S. Department of Education. Interest will be charged from the date the TEACH grant was disbursed to you or on your behalf.

Iraq and Afghanistan Service Grants

If your child is not eligible for a Pell Grant based on your EFC but meets other Pell Grant eligibility requirements, and if they had a parent or guardian who was a member of the U.S. armed forces and died as a result of military service in Iraq or Afghanistan after 9/11, they may be eligible for this grant. There are some restrictions, such as they had to be younger than 24 years old or enrolled in college at least part time at the time of the parent or guardian's death. The award amount is equal to the Pell Grant, but may be reduced due to budget cuts.

Federal Work-Study (FWS) Program

This program provides part-time employment opportunities to students to help fund their education. Roughly 3,400 post-secondary institutions participate in the program, and students must be paid at least minimum wage for their work. Undergraduate students are paid hourly, while graduate students are paid either by the hour or a salary. Either way, the school must pay FWS workers directly at least once a month, unless the student has requested the money be sent to their bank account or applied to education-related expenses. The amount earned cannot exceed the FWS award.

The school pays half the student's wages, and the FWS program covers the rest. The school determines which opportunities the student will be offered. Students apply for the jobs on campus and may be employed by the school or at a number of other places, including:

- Federal, state, or local public agencies
- Private nonprofit organizations
- Private for-profit organizations
- Community service jobs, such as tutoring schoolchildren, literacy tutors, or emergency preparedness and response

And, of course, federal financial aid also includes subsidized and unsubsidized loans. We'll talk about those in detail in the next chapter.

SEARCHING FOR SCHOLARSHIPS ON YOUR OWN

Ah, scholarships are dreamy. People hand over money just because your child got good grades, has a stellar three-point hoops shot, or wrote a wonderful essay. That may be oversimplifying it a bit, but scholarships are monetary awards that your child typically doesn't have to pay back. Some exceptions may be if your student received the scholarship because they made a commitment, such as following a specific course of study. And if your child has a scholarship awarded for multiple years, they might have to maintain a certain grade point average. Most of the time, however, the money is your child's to use for their education with no strings attached.

Your child may receive some scholarships upon graduation from high school based on their achievements. Sometimes, they are awarded because your child has been nominated by the faculty, and you are surprised at the graduation ceremony. Your child may have applied for a scholarship from a local group like the Kiwanis or Lions Club, the Reserve Officers' Training Corps (ROTC), or a local bank or business. Amounts of these scholarships can vary widely, but all are quite helpful in covering the gap between college costs and financial aid. Even a smaller scholarship of a few hundred dollars can help offset some of the costs of textbooks or living expenses.

Those are the most obvious scholarships, but your search should not end there. That is why I advocate starting as early as possible in the high school career to search for scholarships and to keep it up right through your child's college years. If your child is not eligible for a particular award until a certain time, make a note of the application deadline and requirements so you don't forget about it. Many parents and students stop searching for scholarships by December of the senior year, but there are numerous late-deadline scholarships that you can apply for almost right up to the time classes begin. Each scholarship has individual deadlines and requirements, so develop a calendar to make sure you have time to prepare whatever is necessary, submit, and then provide any supplemental information that may be requested.

In Search of Scholarships

One question I often receive is: "Where do we look for scholarships?" My answer: "Everywhere!" Scholarships are available from a wide variety of sources. Here are a few ways you can unearth the dough.

Start at the Guidance Counselor's Office

Your child's guidance counselor should have a complete list of local and other scholarships available, as well as the requirements for securing them. Scholarships may have a variety of requirements, such as meeting certain GPA requirements, planning a major in a particular field of study, or being from a certain geographic area. A good guidance counselor will be able to steer your child toward scholarships that may be the right fit for their student profile and plans.

Ask Everyone You Know

Friends, family members, fellow soccer parents, and more are all potential sources of information when it comes to landing scholarships. Ask co-workers—and, in some cases, your human resources office, since some companies award scholarships to employees' children. You may find leads at your local bank or credit union, church or temple, and civic and charitable organizations. Watch the local newspaper for scholarship awards and note them for your own student. Minority students, children of veterans, students with specific medical conditions, and students entering certain professions may be eligible for various scholarships. You might be surprised at how much is available just because you asked.

Scour Online Opportunities

This is definitely the type of search for which the Internet was invented, but beware of online services that charge to conduct a scholarship search or require you to do something in exchange. There is never a reason to pay a fee, and none of the services are able to guarantee that you will be awarded a scholarship. Here are some reputable college scholarship search sites:

- **BigFuture by College Board** (www.bigfuture. collegeboard.org/scholarship-search): Every year the College Board conducts a Survey of Financial Aid Programs that are available around the country. You can benefit from this work by searching through their information on scholarships, other financial aid, and internships from more than 2,200 programs, totaling nearly $6 billion. Enter as much information as you can to find the most possible matches.
- **U.S. Department of Education** (https://studentaid. ed.gov/sa/types/grants-scholarships): This listing of state grant agencies provides free information on grants, scholarships, and other financial aid for college students available from the state level, including federally supported state programs.
- **CareerOneStop** (www.careeronestop.com): This U.S. Department of Labor website helps you search through more than 7,000 scholarships, fellowships, loans, and other financial aid opportunities. Search by award type, residence preferences, study level, and affiliations.
- **Scholarships.com** (www.scholarships.com): This free service has already helped students search 2.7 million local, state, and national college scholarships and grants worth more than $1.9 billion.

- **Discover Student Loans** (www.discover.com/student-loans/scholarships): The student loan section of Discover's website includes a free scholarship search tool that scours 3 million scholarship opportunities worth more than $18 billion.
- **Chegg** (www.chegg.com/scholarships): This well-known textbook rental company has a section on its website that lists more than $1 billion in awards. Personalized matches are available for students in high school, college, graduate school, and other programs.

Look for Corporate Scholarships
Many corporations believe scholarships are a great way of garnering publicity while providing funds to educate the next generation of employees. Search websites of companies in your child's field of study to determine if scholarships are available.

Ask at Chosen Schools
Merit, endowed, and specialty scholarships may be available through the college or other school you choose. It's a good idea to check with the financial aid and admissions offices to see what opportunities are available. The school may also have scholarship information on its website.

Search for Late-Deadline Scholarships
If you have some extra time, it will be well worth the effort to keep looking online for new scholarship opportunities. New possibilities are announced all the time. If you find a

scholarship from last year that looked like a possibility, find out if it is being offered again this year. Search under "late deadline scholarships," and you will be amazed at the leads you can find. Get creative in how you search. Announce your search on your social media networks, or form a group to share leads with other local parents. Some companies even run scholarship contests, where you don't have to do anything but provide an email and enter.

Get Money for Your Child's Passions
There are a number of scholarships for surprising skills. You may think your child is wasting time playing video games all day, but that could be the ticket to a scholarship to Chicago's Robert Morris University, which offers an athletic scholarship for gamers. Scholarships are available for skills as diverse as being a golf caddy, science whiz, math phenomenon, history aficionado, or artistic genius. Your child can get awards for reading, loving animals, building battle bots, knitting, speaking in public, or making the most creative prom dress. Some partial athletic scholarships are available just for pursuing sports, without having to excel in them. (For information on those "full-ride" athletic scholarships, see "About Those Athletic Scholarships.") There are scholarships for overcoming obstacles in life or living with certain medical issues. Application requirements vary from writing an essay to participating in a competition, so make sure you leave lots of preparation time. No matter what your child is involved in or passionate about, chances are good there is a scholarship for that!

About Those Athletic Scholarships

Your child is the best soccer player your town has ever seen or pitches like nobody's business. So, paying for college is solved—a sports scholarship is on the horizon!

There is so much misinformation about athletic scholarships that it's hard to know where to begin. According to the NCAA, out of the roughly 8 million students who play some sort of sport in high school, a little more than one-sixteenth of them go on to play in college, let alone get merit aid for doing so. While a child may excel in a local or regional program, the pool of competition is much deeper when it's national in scope. In addition, while many people think "athletic scholarship" means "full ride," in cases where aid is awarded—either as an athletic scholarship or some other form of merit aid—often it's just a fraction of the overall COA.

It's also important to consider that playing competitive sports in college is a tremendous commitment that can take time away from studies. If a student is playing a competitive program, it's difficult to hold a part-time job or participate in a work-study program. Be sure to consider the odds and sacrifices before banking on getting money for playing sports in college.

Applying for Scholarships

Once your family has found scholarship opportunities, approach the process the same way you did when applying to schools. Be serious, know the deadlines, and keep track of application requirements. It's a good idea for your student to handle the applications when possible—and some may require essays the student must write. Encourage your child to gather items that may be needed in advance so you're not running around right before the deadline:

- Keep a copy of the FAFSA handy, since some may require financial information.
- Get letters of recommendation together.
- Make copies of high school transcripts.
- Gather several good student photos, either digital or printed (depending on whether the submission must be sent via email or postal service)

It's also a good idea to have a "base essay." This generic essay includes your student's goals and what makes them unique. Then they should do a little research on the sponsoring organization so answers can be tailored appropriately.

If your student has most of these materials available, then they can often make minor modifications to tailor the packet and get it off to the scholarship decision-makers. It is a lot of work, but it is much better than borrowing more money than necessary through student loans.

YOU'VE DONE THE WORK—NOW WHAT?

You've filled out the FAFSA, done your homework about the types of financial aid for which you might qualify, and your student has been applying for scholarships like crazy. Now, the financial aid offers will start coming in.

Unless your student applied for an early action or early decision admission, the acceptance notices and financial aid award packages should start coming in around March or April of your child's senior year. In some cases, even students who receive early action or early decision acceptances may not get their packages until March. Timing depends on the school, so be sure your student checks their prospective schools to find out their schedules. Usually students have until the beginning of May to make a decision, but double-check all deadlines, just to be sure. Review the COA for each school so you can compare them against each other. Be sure to read the financial aid award letter closely, and make sure you understand how much is scholarship and grant money, how much will be covered through the work-study program, and how much you can borrow through federal parent and student loans. Discuss with the admissions or financial aid staff whether the grant and scholarship money your child is receiving may be available for the full four years and what criteria will need to be met to increase the possibility of the award being renewed.

Subtract the scholarships and grants each college is offering. Once you see the amount your family will need to contribute, you may realize your child will also need to chip in financially through part-time work. Make sure you discuss that expectation with your child, as well as how much you want them to contribute. The remaining amount is your out-of-pocket costs for each college. This money will usually come from savings accounts, additional income sources, various federal student loans, or private student loans. Then, it's time to add a few more things to your to-do list.

- **Check the stats.** For each college on your child's list, compare the total COA to the graduation rate and post-graduation employment record. The school should be able to provide data on the percentage of students in their preferred major who graduate in four years, as well as the percentage who obtain employment within six months to a year after graduation. Many can also provide average starting salary information. While looking at these numbers isn't a guarantee, it can help you determine how strong the program is. If the majority of students are graduating in four years and securing employment soon after college, that's a good sign the program is strong and employers are interested in its graduates. A school that costs a bit more but has a higher placement rate at a higher average salary within six months after graduation may deliver a better return on investment (ROI). Of course, remember that many of these numbers are self-reported. While colleges try not to be misleading, their idea of successful job placement may not be the same as your child's.

If your child's favorite college comes up a little low on the financial aid scale, contact the school and ask why the offer was different from the others you received. You may also be able to negotiate your aid package (see "You May Be Able to Negotiate Aid Packages"). Once you have compared the colleges financially, you can think about intangible factors such as the cost of living in the area of the college, typical campus life, personal expenses, and distance from home. Keep in mind that if you live in Chicago and your student wants to go to school in Southern California, the cost of airfare and shipping their stuff across the country is going to add to your overall COA.

You May Be Able to Negotiate Aid Packages

Many people don't know that you can contact the financial aid officer to clarify details about the financial aid package your child was offered. This may be particularly useful if you have different financial aid offers from other schools. Contacting the financial aid office is the key to understanding the offer and seeing if you qualify for other money.

Financial aid officers at the college can give you clear, concise information. Offers from different schools may not be apples-to-apples—they may have different criteria for selecting students and awarding aid, as well as different financial resources—but the officer can walk you through the award you were offered and answer your questions. In some cases, such meetings can result in a more favorable award, especially if you can provide more information about your need or a change in your financial situation.

When you're contacting the school's financial aid officers, remember one simple tip: Be nice. Financial aid officers field many calls from parents asking for more money, and they really do want the best for all students. Being courteous and pleasant can go a long way toward making the interaction go well.

- **Continue searching for scholarships.** Remember, there are late-deadline scholarships available, so it's never too late to look. Even a small scholarship might be helpful for buying books or paying out-of-pocket costs.
- **Make student loan decisions.** After your child chooses a college, you will have to determine how you will pay for those college and living expenses that were not covered by financial aid. If you don't

have enough available in savings, investigate federal and private student loans. Before you do that, parents and students must sit down and talk about how much money will be borrowed and who will be responsible for repaying these loans. We'll dive into that next.

THE BOTTOM LINE

- Financial aid typically comes in the form of grants, scholarships, work-study programs, or loans.
- There are many federal, state, local, and private sources of aid, including scholarships.
- When it comes to seeking various scholarships, grants, and other forms of aid, look everywhere, but start with the guidance counselor's office and online.
- Treat scholarship applications as seriously as college applications. Be prepared and read the guidelines carefully. Every dime you get in scholarships may be one less you need to borrow.

Are Student Loans a Savior or a Sinkhole?

BOBBY MARTIN WAS A GOOD STUDENT with all the attributes a college seeks. He was involved in the community and a good athlete, and held down a part-time job to help pay for his schooling. When it came to choosing a school, only one had the combination of animation and engineering he sought for a career in developing video games. He applied single-choice early decision and was accepted. He and his parents, Joan and Eric, were delighted.

Rather, they were delighted until they saw the $20,000 difference between what the university costs and what Joan and Eric could afford to pay. The only option for him to attend was to take out student loans to cover the difference.

The Martins had very mixed emotions. On one hand, this school could be the ticket to Bobby landing in his dream career. On the other hand, graduating with $80,000 worth of debt—plus interest—was going to make life as a young professional very difficult. They didn't know what to do.

It might seem like a fairy tale come true for many people. A student has a dream of attending college, and the fairy princess—let's call her Banker-belle—comes along and magically grants the money, in the form of student loans, to make that dream come true. Since some lenders will defer payment until graduation, it feels like you and your child don't even have to think about what might happen down the road. Just borrow and study—repeating as needed. Unfortunately, we don't live in a fairy-tale world. No matter how you or your child borrows money, whether it's a credit card, mortgage, personal loan, or student loan, at some point it comes time to pay the piper.

Student loans are a very serious financial responsibility. They are not a gift from Uncle Sam or your local bank. They are loans from lenders that expect to be paid back with interest at some point down the road. The repercussions for not paying are quite serious. The loan could be referred to a collection agency, and your credit history, as well as your child's, could be negatively affected. In the case of federal student loans, future paychecks could be garnished or tax refunds could be withheld. The student, parent, or co-signer on the loan could be held liable if the primary debtor does not make payments.

I have seen many instances where student loans have indeed been a savior. They provided that last little bit of money that allowed a student to attend a favored college without having to give up on the dream. With reasonable care about the amount borrowed, conversation about repayment, and savvy financial planning, the student and the parents were able to manage repayments without putting a severe crimp into the family budget.

On the other hand, I have also seen student loans become a sinkhole for too many families. They borrowed the maximum amount available and spent it foolishly. They had no conversation or prior thought about repayment and didn't go into career fields where they could earn enough money to repay their loans. This is what you see trumpeted in the media on a regular basis and why so many pundits are concerned about a "student loan bubble," similar to the real estate market collapse a few years ago. Students graduate with tens of thousands of dollars of debt and no real career prospects, and are shocked to find out how much it will cost to repay the loans they lived on for four or more years. They start their adult lives with a huge debt burden, can't get loans for cars or homes, and feel their student loans dragging them down as they try to go on and start their own families.

NOT ALL STUDENT LOANS ARE THE SAME

There are two broad types of student loans: federal and private. There are some significant differences between these two categories and varieties of loans within each. Carefully study the financial aid award letter you receive from any colleges your student is considering. Look for anything that says "Direct Subsidized Loan," "Direct Unsubsidized Loan," or "Direct PLUS Loan." These are all different types of federal student loans and will have to be repaid. Always refer to the U.S. Department of Education's website at www.studentaid.ed.gov for the most current information on these programs, but here is some overall information on each:

- **Direct Subsidized Loans:** These are available to undergraduate students with financial need. The amount you may borrow may not exceed your financial need, as determined by the school's analysis of your FAFSA. The U.S. Department of Education currently pays the interest on these loans while the student is in school at least half-time, for the first six months after the student leaves school, and during any period of deferment.
- **Direct Unsubsidized Loans:** These are available to undergraduate and graduate students, but there is no requirement to demonstrate financial need. The student is responsible for paying the interest on these loans. Interest may accrue during the time the student is in school, but the student may choose to accumulate the interest until after graduation and add it on to the principal repayment amount.

There is a loan fee on these types of loans. The loan fee is calculated as a percentage of the loan amount and is proportionately deducted from each loan disbursement. Other types of federal student loans include:

- **Direct PLUS Loans:** These are federal loans that are made to graduate students and parents of dependent undergraduate students. They may be used to pay for education expenses that are not covered by other types of financial aid. There is also a fee for this type of loan. The parent or the graduate student is responsible for payment of this loan.

The student must make sure to remain eligible for any financial aid programs. For federal student loans, this requires completing the FAFSA every year, continuing to meet the basic eligibility criteria, and making satisfactory academic progress. Failure to make satisfactory progress could not only result in loss of financial aid, but it could also result in the student being placed on academic probation or worse.

PRIVATE STUDENT LOANS

If you still need to borrow money toward a college education, private student loans are a helpful option, but there may be differences in fees, interest rates, variable vs. fixed interest, repayment options, prepayment penalty fees, and consolidation opportunities. Always get information from two or three lenders and then compare them to one another so you can make the best choice for your situation. Before doing any research, you will need to understand a few basic concepts about borrowing:

- **Fixed and variable interest rates:** Interest is additional money that is paid to a student loan lender in addition to the original amount of the loan. Fixed interest rates remain the same throughout the life of the loan. If an interest rate is variable, it can change during the course of the loan. Some private student loan lenders might try to attract your attention with lower initial interest rates, but these could increase dramatically as the loan gets older, depending on the current market for interest rates.

- **Interest accrual:** This is the amount of interest that builds on to the student loan. With Direct Subsidized Loans, the federal government is paying this interest. For other federal and private student loans, interest may be accruing the entire time the student is in college. It may be deferred until payment on the principal is due, but that can add up to a substantial amount of money, depending on the interest rate and amount of time the student spends in school.

- **Deferment:** Most federal and private student loans give borrowers the opportunity to defer payment until after graduation, but some private lenders may require payment to begin immediately.

- **Credit check:** Most federal loans do not require a credit history. Private student loans do, which may result in a higher interest rate or stricter repayment terms. To counteract this, student borrowers may need a co-signer on private student loans. Although co-signers are responsible for the life of the loan, having one increases the likelihood of acceptance— and a lower interest rate.

- **Consolidation:** Federal student loans may be combined into a Direct Consolidation Loan, which may make it easier to handle repayment. Private student loans will vary on their ability to be consolidated.

- **Fees:** Always find out if there are fees involved with the student loans you are considering. Some lenders do not charge fees, like Discover Student Loans. If there are fees, they should be clearly spelled out. You should also ask whether there is any type of penalty for early payment.

A FAIRY TALE FOR THE REAL WORLD

While some are fortunate enough to have been born into wealthy families or are talented enough to receive full scholarships, for the rest of us college should be a partnership between parent and child. And the reality is that borrowing decisions have decades-long consequences, so they need to be made carefully and objectively. Yes, you want your child to attend the best possible school. No, it's not all your responsibility. Your child is becoming an adult and is entitled to adult discussions about the financial aspect of attending college. No matter how much they "really, really, really" want to attend a certain school, sometimes the answer has to be "no," "not now," or "let's think about how we can do this." What do you do if your student has their heart set on a particular school and you're not sure you can afford it?

- **Talk to your student.** Remind them how proud you are of this achievement and say that you want to make it happen, but you need to work together. Explain your family's financial situation, and talk about the role you expect your child to play in repaying any loans. How much work is your child willing to do? What sacrifices will your child make to attend this school?

- **Talk to the financial aid office.** You never know. Explain your situation in-depth, tell them how much your child wants to attend, and ask if there is anything that can be done.
- **Maximize those scholarships.** Reread the last chapter and make sure you are doing everything possible to maximize the amount of "free" money you receive.
- **Determine who is capable of earning money.** Starting right now, who is capable of earning extra money? Don't wait until next year or some point in the unspecified future. Who can earn money right now? Every dollar earned is one less dollar that has to be borrowed. There are part-time jobs, online jobs, and network marketing business opportunities like Avon and Tupperware. Whoever has an interest in this dream should be working for the money to pay for it. Your child should try to qualify for a work-study program at school. If not, look for part-time jobs on campus or in local businesses. Long breaks and summer vacations should be opportunities to work as well.
- **Control costs and only borrow what is needed.** The school may be estimating some of the expenses and granting loans based on that amount. Try to find out how much of the cost of attendance is hard costs that

are actually due for tuition and school fees, and then look at the other expenses to see if there is a way to lower them. If they are estimating room and board, maybe your student can live off campus with roommates and share expenses. If the college is including a meal plan, your student can save money by cooking or planning meals wisely. Try not to pay full price for textbooks whenever possible. Find out if there are online or used versions available at a lower cost. Fully break down the expenses and understand what is involved. Even though the school says a certain amount of federal student loans is available, you may not have to borrow that entire amount.

- **Control spending.** If your student does not know how to live on a budget, it is time to learn. One big mistake many students make is taking their student loans and using them for living expenses. Try to borrow money only for actual college costs, and find other ways to pay for living expenses. Look at the family's budget and the student's to come up with a monthly spending amount. Get your student's buy-in that they will do what it takes to live within this budget.

- **Look for other ways to get credit.** Does it have to be an entire four-year experience at this college, or are there some alternatives? Are there high school advanced placement (AP) classes that can be used for college credit? Does a local community college offer courses that could help defray some of the costs involved in taking core subjects? Is your student willing to forgo certain learning activities, such as a semester abroad program, that might provide a more enriching learning experience? Most important, make sure your child knows exactly how much you are willing to pay yearly and for exactly how many years. At the undergraduate level, this should only be two to four years so your child is motivated to perform well. Talk now about whether your student thinks they may need a post-graduate or doctoral degree and how you will pay for that.

- **Get that buy-in.** This may be the first time you have talked to your student on such an adult level, and it might come as quite a shock. Explain what sacrifices you are willing to make and what sacrifices you expect your child to make. If they are not willing to participate fully, then the "dream" school may not be a reality.

SHOULD YOU STILL BORROW?

Even after you have squeezed every last penny out of scholarships and your household budget, you might still have to borrow money. Try to borrow as little as possible, and keep track of how much you are borrowing. Use a student loan repayment calculator to figure out how much the payments are going to be after graduation, and add on new loans as they come along. Then talk to the admissions office to find out how many of their graduates are obtaining jobs in their desired field, and what kind of starting salaries they are earning. Even the best university is no good if your child cannot earn enough money to repay any loans.

I typically advise students to borrow no more than what they project their first-year salary will be. For example, if they think their starting salary will be about $40,000, I typically encourage them to take out no more than $40,000 in student loans. (For more recommendations, see "Resources from Discover.")

You must have a very clear understanding with your child of who will be responsible for repayment of all student loans after graduation, especially if you have signed your name to any of them. Payment notices will start arriving within six months, and there should be a plan in place to begin repayment. If your child scores a high-paying job, everything might be fine. But if your family is like most, graduates start at lower-salary jobs, and the student ends up returning to the nest for an extended period of time. You may want to talk about those expectations now, especially since costs for a car, health insurance, and food can add an extra burden to the family's budget. It's common today for young professionals to marry a partner with student loans, which puts double the financial pressure on the newlyweds' budget.

I'll cover more about student loans in the next section, but some parents also wonder if they should borrow from other sources to help finance their child's college education. This can be quite risky and will really involve a high level of discussion with your student about repayment responsibilities. For the most part, I do not recommend borrowing against a credit card to pay for college expenses. Usually, these have very high interest rates, involve revolving credit balances, and have very few repayment options.

Resources from Discover

For years, I've worked with Discover Student Loans as their Brand Ambassador. While I don't typically recommend specific brands, Discover has some impressive tools for parents and students to help them understand available options on how to pay for college. Some of these include:

- **CollegeCovered.com** (www.collegecovered.com): Use the free interactive tool for guidance with completing the FAFSA. You can also find videos and articles to help you and your student with planning and paying for college.

- **Student loan calculators** (www.discover.com/student-loans/calculators.html): You can use the student loan calculators to figure out how much to borrow and estimate monthly loan payments for your student's education.

- **College major comparison** (www.discover.com/student-loans/majors): Compare the average median salaries of graduates for over 170 college majors to help your student understand the economic prospects of their chosen field.

Some parents ask if they should take out a line of credit against their home to finance their child's education. However, doing so carries risk if the line of credit can't be repaid. Interest rates are usually reasonable, but payments begin right away. Other parents want to know if they should dip into their retirement savings. The answer depends on several factors, such as the parents' age now and upon their child's graduation. There may be early withdrawal penalties and tax consequences to pulling money out of a qualified retirement plan. Plus, retirement accounts are not taken into consideration when calculating financial aid eligibility. Putting that money into liquid assets might do more damage to your financial aid award.

Is college worth it? In most cases, the answer is still "yes." As I said previously, time and time again, it has been shown that people with college degrees earn more than their cohorts with a high school education. The secret is to balance the risk with the reward. Think ahead, make sound money decisions, and don't let your heart rule the decision-making process.

THE REALITIES OF STUDENT LOANS

So, your student has their heart set on going to Really Expensive University, which is about $20,000 more per year than you can afford. For the sake of calculation, let's say they graduate in four years, accruing $80,000 in student loan debt in the following combination of subsidized and unsubsidized loans:

- *Direct Subsidized Loans:* $23,000 at a 4.29 percent interest rate
- *Direct Unsubsidized Loans:* $8,000 at a 4.29 percent interest rate
- *Private Student Loans:* $49,000 at a 6.15 percent interest rate

The total amount your student will repay is a whopping $103,902 with a standard 120-month repayment plan. The payment will be $865.85 per month! Let's say the starting salary at the job your child gets right out of college is $40,000 and they live in California, where the state income tax is 2.91 percent. Your child's take-home pay after all standard deductions will be roughly $2,400 per month.[6] They will be spending more than one-third of their take-home pay on repaying student loans!

That's an awfully heavy burden to carry as your child starts their career. And if your student plans on going to graduate school, that can add tens of thousands of dollars more onto that loan balance. Your child is tying themselves to these payments for roughly 10 years, unless they prepay the loans. Is this really the best course of action?

REPAYING STUDENT LOANS

Most student loan payments start about six months after graduation, so parents and students need to plan ahead to make sure those monthly payments are incorporated into the family budget. The government offers many options for repayment, including income-based plans. Here are some terms you need to know about repaying student loans:

- **Loan consolidation:** By the time a student graduates, there may be 10 or more different student loans that need to be repaid. Since this can get confusing, it can sometimes be beneficial to consolidate loans so there will only be one payment to make each month. A Direct Consolidation Loan allows the borrower to combine multiple federal education loans into one

How Much Should We Borrow?

Discussing the cost of school and how much your family can afford can be difficult. However, avoiding the conversation and borrowing without careful consideration of your family's ability to repay, as well as clear expectations about who will pay what, can lead to very bad decisions and long-term financial consequences. Here are some talking points to go over with your student:

- Look at the average employment rate six months after graduation and the average starting salary in your student's major. Use a site like TaxFormCalculator.com to get a good understanding of what your student's take-home pay might be when they get a job after completing school.

- Use the federal repayment estimator at StudentLoans.gov (https://studentloans.gov/myDirectLoan/mobile/repayment/repaymentEstimator.action), enter the amounts of the various loans you will need and their interest rates, and determine an estimate of your total repayment amount with interest, as well as the monthly payment. The site also shows you various repayment options offered by the federal government. It's important for your family to be clear about who will be responsible for making those payments.

- Discuss the challenges of the job market and what will happen if they don't get a job right away, as well as other potential pitfalls, such as if your student does not complete their degree in four years.

- Look at possibilities for reducing the overall cost, such as attending community college for a year or two and transferring, or completing their degree in less than four years.

loan. There can be differences between federal and private student loans, so it will be necessary to check with private lenders regarding loan consolidation opportunities.

There are pros and cons to loan consolidation, because it may result in the loss of some benefits. Since repayment terms may be longer, you might end up repaying more money in the long run. You can also lose some benefits that were associated with the original loan, such as interest rate discounts, principal rebates, or some loan cancellation benefits.

- **Deferment and forbearance:** Defaulting is failure to make payment on student loans. To avoid this, the borrower may be able to qualify for a deferment or forbearance. With deferment, you can temporarily delay repayment of the principal and interest on your loan. Borrowers are responsible for paying the interest that accumulates on subsidized, unsubsidized, and PLUS loans during the deferment period, but payment is not due until the deferment period ends.

    If you don't qualify for a deferment, you may qualify for forbearance, which could allow you to stop making payments or reduce your monthly payment for up to 12 months. Interest continues to accrue on both subsidized and unsubsidized loans. Borrowers may be eligible for forbearance due to financial hardship, illness, medical residency, certain teaching programs, or military service. Deferment and forbearance opportunities may vary with private student loan lenders, so always ask questions before signing.

- **Loan forgiveness, cancellation, and discharge:** In most cases, student loans cannot be discharged in a bankruptcy. But, there are some situations where the borrower is not be required to repay the student loans. Conditions differ between federal and private student loans but may include death, disability, teacher loan forgiveness, and public service forgiveness. Always check with your lender if you are having difficulty repaying any student loans.

THE BOTTOM LINE

- Student loans are a big responsibility with serious financial consequences if they are not repaid. Borrowing should not be taken lightly.
- Not all student loans are the same. Know the difference between federal and private loans, as well as the difference between subsidized and unsubsidized loans, which can make a big difference in the amount your student needs to repay.
- Look at the real numbers before borrowing by using calculators to determine repayment amounts and estimated take-home pay to determine the realities of student loan payment impact. Large amounts of loan debt could show up on a credit report and possibly make it more difficult for the student to obtain new credit, including a mortgage.
- With few exceptions, the name of your college means little in the real world. Think about whether borrowing to go to an expensive school is worth it. After all, those tens—or even hundreds—of thousands of dollars can go a long way toward a secure financial future.

PART 3
OFF AND AWAY

Why Can't Freshmen Manage Their Money Better?

ELISE MARTIN THOUGHT HER SON, TOMMY, had a good understanding of money before he left for college. He had worked part-time at a local supermarket during high school and managed to save several thousand dollars toward his college expenses. He was diligent about looking for scholarships, and he had chosen a school where he wouldn't have to borrow too much money to attend. Elise had actually patted herself on the back silently when she heard other parents complain about their children not appreciating the sacrifices it took to send them to college.

But once Tommy got to his university campus, it seemed like all those good habits went out the window. He blew through the balance of his student loan funds in a couple of months. He signed up for three different credit cards at a school fair where card issuers were exhibiting. Then, he racked up several thousand dollars in debt. Elise was terrified of how much Tommy had spent and the fact that it was jeopardizing whether the family would be able to afford for him to complete school.

It's a sad fact that many students never learn how to manage their money before heading off to college. Perhaps their parents weren't effective at instilling good financial habits, or these students didn't believe what their parents had to say. In any case, freshman year turns out to be a big adjustment time.

Two different factors come into play that can contribute to a difficult financial situation for the new freshman. Sending a child to college in the first place can really put a strain on the family's budget. Consequently, Mom and Dad have less financial flexibility and aren't as likely to pass out money whenever they are asked. They may be looking at younger siblings who are talking about college, or thinking about their own retirement needs. So, a student who thinks that "low balance" means "ask Mom and Dad for more money" is often in for a rude awakening.

Combine that with a college student who thinks that they already know everything, and the problem is magnified a thousand times. Students who may have been chafing under strict financial rules at home finally feel like they can buy whatever they want whenever they want, without realizing the financial repercussions. There may be student loan money in an account for living and school expenses that was intended to last a semester, or they could have access to credit cards without their parents' knowledge. So, they buy a few things for the dorm room, party a little longer, and generally spend money until the bills start coming in and they realize there might be a problem. They go back to their parents, who have a choice about what to do. Do they give their child the money and hope a lesson has been learned, or try to nip this bad habit in the bud? It's not an easy choice, so here are a few ways you might be able to help your student overcome a poor decision-making process.

MONEY MANAGEMENT FOR THE COLLEGE FRESHMAN

It's probably not a good idea to take all control of money back from your student. First, it might not be possible now that your student is 18 and legally an adult. But, worse, rescinding their responsibility does not provide any usable life skills. Instead, it only delays the lessons until after graduation, giving them four more years of opportunity to make bad financial decisions.

While racking up debt and spending money unwisely can be upsetting for parents or guardians who may need to lend a hand in cleaning up the mess, such a misstep can also provide a valuable learning opportunity. Of course, the goal is to head off this kind of trouble before it begins. However, if your student is struggling with money management, consider these tips to help them become more financially responsible.

- **Look at your own situation first.** Sometimes the apple doesn't fall far from the money tree. Take a good look at how you spend money personally, and honestly decide whether you are setting a good example for your child.

- o Have you refinanced a mortgage to pay off debts?
- o Are your credit cards maxed out?
- o Do you finance purchases you can't afford?
- o Do you have a sufficient amount of money saved for the proverbial "rainy day"?

Parents are always the first place a child looks to learn about making financial choices. If you are not using money wisely, how do you ever expect that your student will learn to do so? As part of your discussion, let your student know what you might have done wrong, and what you plan to do to get your own financial house in order. You can challenge each other to make changes, and keep each other motivated as time goes by.

- **Calculate the debt together.** Have an open and honest money conversation with your freshman. You might have to promise that you will not get upset, but you need a full understanding of the situation. First, list all the student loans that have already been borrowed by you and your student. Explain that interest builds on these loans during the college years, and use a repayment calculator to estimate monthly payment amounts after graduation. Let your student know how much, if anything, you plan to contribute toward repaying these loans. Then look at the credit card debt that may have already accumulated. Talk about how quickly interest increases the amount owed, and show your student that late fees and penalties can really add to the outstanding balance. Move on to other expenses your student may have acquired, such as cell phone and data plans.

- **Honestly discuss your money sources.** Your student may be shocked to see how much money needs to be paid on a monthly basis now, and how much debt is projected for the future. Your family may already be under a financial strain to come up with necessary tuition payments every year. Show your student how much you are spending on college and family expenses, and explain there is no room left in the family budget. Reinforce that any accumulated debt is going to be your student's responsibility now and in the future.
- **Draw up a budget—again.** Yes, again. You probably tried to give your student a budget before the semester began, but the lesson obviously didn't sink in. So, take a deep breath, and start over now that you may have a little more of their attention. Reinforce the ideas of income and expenses, and show your student how much money is available to spend every month, including the new debt payments. There are only two ways to change this budget—either your student can find a way to earn more through jobs or scholarships, or spend less on day-to-day costs.
- **Explain your expectations.** You may need to pull in the reins a little so your student is not spending completely unfettered, but you can't take over all control and dole out money like you did when your child was in grammar school. Explain the amount you are willing to provide as an allowance every

month, and let your child know what will happen if spending exceeds that amount. Your child may need to cut back on smartphone use, find a job, or forgo spring break plans. There should also be the expectation of summer jobs to earn money. And remember to tell your student how much of the student loans you expect to pay after graduation and how much will be their responsibility.

- **Provide an incentive.** Instead of just handing out money, perhaps you can provide a little incentive for your student to earn it. You might want to come up with some type of reward you can offer if your student gets good grades, increases income, or decreases debt. Set realistic goals together, and then stick to your guns. If your student does not meet the goal, there should not be a reward. Discuss what went wrong, set new goals, and try again.

- **Keep at it.** It's an old story, but it's still possible that your student will continue their wild spending ways. It is your job to keep on top of the situation, and be resolute in your teaching. Keep the topic on the table, continue the analysis, offer suggestions, and be a cheerleader for your student. If something goes right, make sure you acknowledge the progress, and work together to decide what steps need to be taken next.

Should you pay your student's debt to "get over the hump"? That is a tricky question. While it can make your student's life much easier now, it might not provide lessons down the line. Your student may act contrite and make all kinds of promises, but forget everything once the next semester begins or a tempting spending offer presents itself. You need agreement on a very specific set of actions before you pay the debt completely and on the consequences if there is no follow-through.

You might consider paying the debt as a loan, which your student will have to repay to you. Charge interest, and be realistic about how much money your student can give you every month. Agree on what happens if this payment schedule is not met.

THE HARD FACTS ABOUT POOR MONEY MANAGEMENT

Your student may feel that once they're out from under your roof, it's time for you to get off their back about money. After all, what's the big deal if they have to borrow a few dollars here and there? They've got 40 or 50 years to repay it, or maybe they won't have to repay it at all. They've seen other families who live on credit cards, leases, and debt, and they seem to be doing just fine, thank you very much. So, why should they suffer?

It's important to help your student dig a bit deeper to see the problems that debt can cause and why they want to avoid them.

Not Paying Student Loans

This is a big one, especially with federal student loans. If federal student loans are not paid, the government can and will garnish borrowers' paychecks and will even withhold federal tax refunds to which the borrower might otherwise be entitled. Private student loan lenders can turn delinquent accounts over to outside collection agencies, which can lead to some pretty intense collection tactics. This will hurt your credit and can make it more difficult and expensive to get everything from a mortgage or credit card to a mobile phone and automobile insurance.

Overusing Credit

Credit cards are so nice and convenient, aren't they? And credit card companies love to court college students. They come onto campus and offer special promotions to get students to sign up for their cards. The student starts using it, and it seems like fun until the bills start arriving. The student spent $100, but the minimum payment is only $25, so that's what they pay. The next month, the student spends another $100, so the balance is now $175, plus interest on the $75 carried over from last month. Now the minimum payment is $30, but that's still not so bad.

But soon the interest is more than the actual merchandise and services charged. The student finds the minimum payment has risen beyond what their budget will allow, so they skip a payment, but the problem is that interest keeps building and late fees are added on too. By the time their parents find out, the student is often in real trouble.

The best solution is to not rely on credit cards. Explain how credit cards work and encourage your student to use cash or debit cards whenever possible. If it can't be paid for in cash, it's not affordable. That's an important lesson for your child now and for life.

Bad Credit Reports

Many students don't learn about credit reports until it's too late. Credit reporting bureaus collect information from credit card companies, utility companies, telephone carriers, collection agencies, and many other sources and compile them into reports on repayment history. It's important to teach your student about the implications of bad credit. Not making payments, paying minimum amounts, skipping payments, or having too much credit are all reported to the various credit bureaus. While this might not seem like a big deal to your student now, having a bad credit rating can cause a lot of harm later in life. It could affect their ability to rent an apartment, purchase auto insurance, buy a home, or get a car. Building a good credit history now will make life after graduation easier for both of you.

Life on the Edge

Today's young adults may see many people living on the edge. They may have watched their parents or their friends' parents use credit all the time, pay minimal amounts, and still seem to be having a pretty good time of it. But then something happens, and living on borrowed money doesn't look so attractive after all. Many families are just one hardship away from financial disaster. It could be something like a medical emergency, job loss, disability, natural disaster, divorce, or unexpected death of a partner, and suddenly the whole apple cart is upset. Sometimes, it might even be due to outside forces, like we recently saw with the economic downturn.

The best insurance against financial havoc is good financial habits. By saving money, spending wisely, keeping debt to a minimum, and building good credit, it's possible to weather even the most difficult financial circumstances—or, at least, make the fallout less severe.

Bankruptcy

Perhaps you have heard of some students who borrowed the maximum amount of money and then declared bankruptcy. They act like this was the smartest decision they ever made—racking up big debt to pay for education, then having most or all of it wiped away.

Your student may have heard about this "tactic" for paying for education, but that story isn't the whole truth. It is very difficult to have federal student loans discharged in bankruptcy. Not only must the borrower be able to prove that they can't pay the loans now, but they must also prove that paying the loans in the future would cause an undue hardship on them and their family. Bankruptcy is a serious financial decision and can make it very difficult to get credit for years. A bankruptcy remains on your credit history for 10 or more years and may even make it difficult to find a job if employers find out.

A Lifelong Lesson

If you have noticed a theme in this book, it's being smart about money. While college is there primarily to impart specific knowledge and skills, it is also a time of transition from teenager to adult. By the time students enter college, they should have a solid foundation of money management skills. They then have four years to practice using these skills on their own, so they will be good financial decision-makers as well as employable adults upon graduation.

The Value Excuse?

There has been some media attention around borrowers who claim that their college didn't deliver an education that would enable them to earn a sufficient amount of money to repay their loans, so they believe they shouldn't have to pay anything and default on their loans. Others say the burden is too heavy, the lenders are at fault for giving them so much money, or it puts a real damper on their lifestyle choices. They default, too.

All of those are excuses and reasons to not take responsibility for your own actions. Don't shift the blame onto others for decisions you made. The consequences of default are the same whether you feel it's justified or not. If your student borrows money and doesn't repay it, their credit will be hurt. If you co-signed on the loan, your credit will be damaged, too.

But the unseen damage is that other people have to pay for their actions in some way. If they suffer losses, lenders may curtail money they are willing to lend, or increase costs to others to make up for the money they lost. In those cases, everyone loses. Be smart about borrowing, for everyone's sake.

There may be ups and downs along the way, but that is all part of the learning process. Think back on how much you knew about handling money when you were just 18 or 19. A college freshman who makes money mistakes isn't destined for a life of money failure. With proper direction and support, you can help your child learn to make sound financial decisions.

Money training begins when your child is young and builds to a crescendo during the college years. The lessons you impart now will have a lifelong impact on whether your child leads a life of debt or financial stability. It may also help in just a few short years when you try to keep your college senior from freaking out about money.

THE BOTTOM LINE

- Even the most level-headed kids can have trouble managing money once they get out on their own.
- Your student may hear a great deal of misinformation about everything from how great credit cards are to how bankruptcy is a solution for student loan debt. You need to take the lead on financial education before harm is done.
- Explain how credit cards work and how interest accumulates. Those minimum payments can get you into a lot of trouble.
- Lead by example. If your student is picking up bad money habits by watching your family in action, it might be time for a little internal housekeeping. Be honest about your mistakes and what you're trying to do to improve your own money management skills.

Financial Reality 101: A Primer for College Seniors

ANNA JENKINS WAS A SENIOR AT HER STATE UNIVERSITY and beginning to make plans to move out on her own. Since she was in high school, she had planned on working in advertising in New York City. Now, she was almost finished with her bachelor's degree and had even managed to save a bit of money toward her goal. But her parents were concerned. She had been watching too many movies and television shows about single people affording enormous Manhattan apartments on their own, when the reality was that she'd likely be able to afford a small place in Queens with a couple of roommates. But every time her parents tried to explain reality to her, she shut down and told them to mind their own business.

MONEY SCHOOL IS NOW IN SESSION

When your "children" are in their 20s and about to finish college, it can feel strange or be downright difficult to have money talks with them. Sometimes, parents are shocked to find out they have raised a financial illiterate. If this was not corrected during the college years, they may now be looking at unleashing this lack of knowledge on the world. An inability to handle a budget or spend student loans wisely does not bode well for managing a salary, mortgage payments, and car loans in the not-so-distant future. It might be time for you to hold your own course: Financial Reality 101.

Even though your son or daughter is technically an adult, the post-college period will likely still have an impact on your family and, possibly, your finances. Your child may land a job right after college, which is great. However, their salary may not be enough to support them, especially if they need to move to an expensive area. Or they may want to live at home for a while to save money. In other scenarios, your student may continue to be a student, choosing graduate school rather than a full-time job. Other students won't be as lucky—they may find it takes a while to land a job, even with an associate's or bachelor's degree or trade school certification, and may end up back in their old bedroom in your home.

Now, you've got another person back under your roof. Your expenses increase for everything from food to utilities. If you go out for a family dinner, there's another person at the table. If you're thinking of downsizing your home, it can be complicated if you have a child who's returned to the nest. And when that six-month grace period has ended and the student loans are coming due, someone is going to have to pay them, or it could affect your credit, too, if you've co-signed for the loans. All these factors have an impact on you and your student's life.

FINANCIAL REALITY 101 FOR THE COLLEGE SENIOR

The next time your student is home for a weekend or a holiday, insist on discussing money, budgeting, and student loans. They may bristle, but this is a good time for you to work on shifting your relationship from one of parent and child to parent and young adult. Discussing money isn't easy, but I hope you've been having some money discussions all along, at least about paying for college, so this territory won't be too unfamiliar. But, even if it is, you'll want to set the tone.

First, spend some time preparing for the discussion. Think about the purpose and the outcome you want. For example, you might have a child who is:

- Moving home, and you want to manage expectations about how long that will last and what expenses the child will be responsible for covering.
- Relocating to a new city and facing new expenses, so you want to be sure they understand how you will and will not help financially.
- Unable to find a job and is moving home, so you want to be clear about what your expectations are while they are job-hunting.
- Saddled with debt that they racked up during school, and they are asking for help paying it off.

Be clear about what you are willing to do—financially and otherwise—to help your child. You might want to draw up an agenda or spreadsheet to cover key points or break down expenses, payments, or debt so you can see the numbers clearly and be sure you're on the same page when it comes to what will need to happen next. (See the "Real-World Living Expenses" worksheet on page 157 for help creating a budget.)

You might also want to have a calculator and a laptop, tablet, or even a smartphone that will let you access debt repayment calculators, such as student loan or credit card payment estimating sites like the repayment estimator at StudentLoans.gov (https://studentloans.gov/myDirect Loan/mobile/repayment/repaymentEstimator.action) or Bankrate.com's Debt Payoff Calculator (www.bankrate.com/calculators/credit-cards/balance-debt-payoff-calculator.aspx). These can help you see the payments your student will need to make and let you compare different payment amounts and how they will affect the total amount that needs to be repaid and the length of time necessary to do so. There are really two areas you want to cover: what your student needs to do financially upon graduation and how to finance an advanced degree if that is on the horizon.

This may be one of the hardest lessons your student will have to learn—and that includes courses in calculus and organic chemistry! However, a solid foundation now could mean the difference between financial success and failure in life. Here are some of the lessons you want to impart while you still have a chance to make an impact on your child's choices.

Real-World Living Expenses

As you sit down to help your young adult figure out what living on their own will cost, consider these line items and add your own based on their situation. Estimate the cost for each to create an estimated monthly budget.

_____ Rent

_____ Utilities (gas, electricity, water, sewer, etc.)

_____ Health insurance

_____ Student loan payments

_____ Car (include payment, maintenance, insurance)

_____ Food

_____ Clothes

_____ Commuting expenses (gas, tolls, public transportation)

_____ Personal care (hair styling, personal grooming services and products, gym membership)

_____ Medical/prescription expenses

_____ Entertainment (dining out, going to movies)

_____ Travel

_____ Miscellaneous

_____ _____

_____ _____   Others

_____ _____   (insert expenses based on personal need/circumstances; for example, add expenses for

_____ _____   pets, hobbies, etc., on which you spend money each month)

_____ _____

_____ **TOTAL**

_____ Gross salary (monthly)

_____ Take-home pay (monthly)

_____ **DIFFERENCE**

MOVING ON . . . HOME

Graduation day is nearing, and it's looking more and more like your student is going to pack up the car and come right back to your house. Whether due to unemployment, enrollment in graduate school, or simply as a plan to save a little money, your nest is going to be fuller again.

When children move home after being away at college, the dynamics can make life difficult. They have been off on their own for four or more years. They typically don't need guardians anymore—they're legally adults. At the same time, this is your home and your wishes should be respected. In addition, it's important for your child to contribute to the household, if not monetarily, by helping you in other ways. It's not unreasonable for you to ask for rent or, if that's not financially possible now, for assistance with other, smaller expenses or even chores for your child to earn their keep.

Lay out these expectations in writing so your son or daughter can see them. If they cannot contribute financially due to unemployment, explain how you expect them to help around the house or with other expenses. You may require that they cook dinner one or two days a week and help with household chores until they get a job, then contribute financially as well.

You may find that other parents are letting their children return home with no such conditions or, worse, are paying for apartments or other living expenses while their child gets on their feet. This is when you need to dip back into those parenting skills you used when they were younger: Your household, your rules. Don't let guilt overcome you.

Your children need to learn to be responsible contributors to the world. If other parents want to enable their children to do nothing, that's not your problem. Set your own boundaries, and don't let them be moved by misplaced guilt.

MOVING AWAY

You're so proud because your student landed a great job in their chosen field, but it requires moving cross-country to an expensive new city. While other parents might be subsidizing rent or living expenses, you're not in a position to do so—or, at least, not entirely.

In situations like this, it's important for your student to understand the realities of monthly living expenses. In addition to rent, food, utilities, phone, and other necessities, they may have to pay for commuting expenses, work clothes, and work-related expenses. Then, there's an apartment that needs to be furnished. And if they want to travel home for holidays or visits, that adds a whole new layer of expenses.

But you raised your child to fly and follow their dreams, so help them create a budget to accommodate this new life. Look at the realities of their expenses—fixed, variable, and one-time. (See an overview of expenses in the "Moving Costs" checklist.)

SLAYING A MONSTER DEBT

If your child comes home with credit card, student loan, or other debt hanging over their head, you may need to add another element to the conversation. This can be frustrating, especially if the debt is much larger than you anticipated after carefully planning and paying for your child's college education for so many years. But it's a critical issue that can affect your child's future for years to come, so it's important to take emotion out of the discussion and deal with the facts so you can get to a solution.

Moving Costs

Moving out is exciting, but it comes with an array of potential expenses. Plan for these before you sign the lease.

_____	First and last month's rent
_____	Security deposit (often equal to one to two times rent)
_____	Utility deposits (if required)
_____	Moving service (or, at least, pizza and beverages for friends who help you move)
_____	Furniture (if unit is unfurnished)
_____	Window coverings
_____	Bedding/towels
_____	Kitchen supplies, cutlery, and cookware
_____	Glasses
_____	Flatware
_____	Cleaning supplies
_____	Others
_____	_____
_____	_____
_____	_____
_____	_____
_____	_____
_____	**TOTAL**

- **Find out how much money is really due.** Take a deep breath, and find out exactly how much debt your college senior is carrying. Your child can search online to find the balance and expected payment amounts on federal student loans, and contact any private lenders to find out the balances on those accounts. Then look at credit card bills, cell phone expenses, and miscellaneous charges that built up at school. Ask your student to be open and honest with you so you can find out the real figure. You may both be shocked by how much debt there is. Write it all down, including interest that's accruing on outstanding balances or balances that may be on the verge of being sent to a collection agency, if things have gotten that bad.

- **Calculate how much money is needed for the rest of the school year.** Look at living and graduation expenses, and find out if there are outstanding college bills that will keep your student from receiving their degree. Some schools won't let your student participate in graduation ceremonies or confer the degree until the final payments are made.

- **Discuss who is paying what.** Have you informed your student how much of the student loans you will be willing to pay? Parents might be facing financial challenges themselves, have other children in college, or be concerned about their own retirement savings, but all too often they fail to share these concerns with their student. Their child is shocked to find out they have absolutely no intention of paying anything on their student loan or credit card debt, and goes into a sudden panic. If you haven't had these discussions already, now is the time.

- **Work the scenarios together.** Now that you know how much money your student owes and what the future is expected to hold, you can help run some financial scenarios. Estimate a monthly payment amount and calculate new expenses under each scenario. Then help your student project how much money will be needed to cover loan payments and living expenses. For example, your child may have $25,000 in student loan and credit card debt that may require monthly payments of roughly $263, depending on interest. Your child says that they want to move out on their own, so you budget rent, transportation, and living expenses of $2,000 per month. That means your child will need to net at least a yearly income of $27,000 after taxes, which means a starting gross salary of more than $30,000, depending on federal and state taxes and other withholding expenses. If this is not realistic, help your student develop alternative scenarios. Perhaps moving home and paying a small rent while trying to make a dent in the debt burden is the solution, or your child may need to find two jobs if they are intent on moving out. You must try to remain objective as the parent and offer advice based solely on the facts, not on what you think your student should be doing.

- **Build a budget.** If the scenarios work out for your student to pursue a given objective, then work together to develop a budget. Help them understand gross and net income, calculate living expenses, and estimate how much money might be left for saving or discretionary spending. (Refer to the "Real-World Living Expenses" worksheet on p age 157 to give you a good framework.)

HEADING OFF TO GRAD SCHOOL

If an advanced degree is looming, that may add an entirely different factor to your equations. While it may mean the possibility of a higher income for your child down the road, it is likely to add even more to the debt load. A few years of grad school can often cost as much as four years in an undergraduate program, and your student could wind up with $50,000, even $100,000 or more, in debt before even beginning a career.

Although a master's degree or doctorate is required for many professions, it is sometimes not cost-effective. Although endowments, grants, and scholarships are available, they are often not enough to cover classes and independent living needs. Many students acquire much larger student loans for grad school and find that the anticipated earning potential just isn't enough. On top of that, although principal payments might be deferred, interest may continue to accrue on certain student loans, making the amount due upon graduation even higher. You and your student need to be certain of the costs and benefits involved in a decision of this nature.

LET'S TALK

Keeping Cool during the Money Talk

Your college graduate may think they know everything. But with big money issues hanging overhead, they still may need you to see their way through. Money discussions, especially when they're about struggles, can be tough. To be effective, you have to keep emotion out of it and get to solutions. Try these approaches, especially if things get heated or your child is resistant.

- **To open the conversation:** "Graduation is coming, and you have some big life changes approaching. Let's set up a time when we can talk about your plans and discuss how you can start on the best financial footing."

  "I'm so excited about your new job. I know this transition—with a new job, home, and financial responsibilities—is going to be exciting. I'd like to talk to you about how we can work together to be sure your financial future is secure."

  "I know you're worried about your debt. I want to help you figure out some solutions. When can we sit down and talk about it?"

- **If things get heated:** "I understand you're no longer a child, and I'm very proud of all you've accomplished. I'm not judging you. I want to work with you as an adult and help you find solutions. What's the best way to do that?"

  "Boy, this is a tough subject, isn't it? It took me until well into adulthood to be able to discuss money issues without getting emotional. I understand how stressful this is. I'm here for you to help you find solutions."

  "I know this is challenging and scary. I love you, and I want to help you find the best solution here. Let's just look at the numbers and see what we can figure out. What do you see as a solution?"

This might not be a conversation that can be completed in just one session. You may need to identify the challenges and then come back later with solutions. But try to keep cool and stay focused on positive outcomes.

Together, you may decide that it is best to put off the advanced degree for a short period of time, while focusing on gaining experience and earning money in the short term. It may be possible to attend part time or take some courses online or at a local college while living at home to save on costs. There must be a realistic expectation of earning enough money before the final decision is made to incur a larger debt load.

This discussion should give your student a solid handle on what it takes to succeed financially, and you should be able to watch them get started on a solid foundation. The one last item that could still be looming over your student's head (and yours if you were a co-signer) is student loans. They can't be ignored, because they could be a part of everyone's life for many years to come.

THE BOTTOM LINE

- Just because your senior has a degree doesn't mean they aced financial basics.
- Once graduation is around the corner, your student may be faced with many tough decisions, including whether or not to move home.
- Setting ground rules up front makes a smoother transition because your student knows what to expect, financially and otherwise.
- Dealing with debt can be an emotional issue. Try to keep the conversation based on the facts. Explosive drama will just get in the way of finding solutions effectively.

11

Paying Back Those Student Loans

ONE OF THE GREAT JOYS OF MY JOB is hearing from the students with whom I've worked. I especially love when they check in after graduation. But when I got a call from Paul White, I was concerned. He told me that he had graduated and found a job and really thought he had a handle on all his expenses. Then, the student loan bills started to roll in. He got behind and couldn't seem to get caught up. He was thinking of defaulting and letting the chips fall where they may. We talked for a while and came up with some solutions, which was a relief for him. I was glad because what he was considering had very serious consequences.

At some point, it seems like it was decided that college graduates were "entitled" to certain things after college—a job, apartment, car, and a booming social life. After all, your student worked hard for that degree and should be able to enjoy the fruits of those labors now, right? But that wasn't a very realistic approach, as the millennial generation—and, following them, generation Z—has discovered. Many graduated from college with little worry about the tens of thousands of dollars in student loans they had racked up and were blindsided by the recession. Too few high-paying jobs were available, affordable housing opportunities disappeared, and the cost of living shot up dramatically.

It would be a really good idea for colleges to teach a "money management in the real world" course, but most of them don't. As a result, tens of thousands of financially unprepared students graduate each year, already thousands of dollars in debt due to credit cards and student loans. The students and their parents become overwhelmed when they try to figure out the best course of action, the payment due notices start to arrive faster than anyone expected, a few payments are delayed or missed, and a small challenge suddenly turns into a huge problem.

What kinds of steps can you take to help your children over this first real financial hurdle in their adult lives? You hate to see them going through difficult times, but it really isn't a good idea to step in and completely take over, either. You may have other children in college, need to save for your own retirement, and be limited in how much help is feasible or advisable. So here are a few things you can do:

KEEP TALKING
If you have built a solid relationship with your child over the high school and college years, there is no need to stop

now. Go ahead and keep talking about money matters, find out how the student loan payments are going, discuss any hard times you might have experienced financially, and share insights about how you were able to overcome those challenges. Even though they are "all grown up" and on their own now, you know that it can still be a little scary to think you are facing the world on your own. Knowing there is the support of a loving parent can make all the difference.

OFFER TO HELP REVIEW THE OPTIONS
Although you may think you covered everything with your child after graduation, ask if you can help go through the options again. Sit down together and review the student loan situation in a nonjudgmental manner. Try not to make accusations or admonitions. Simply get the facts and help assess the current situation, so you can discuss possible options without letting emotions overtake the conversation. Help your graduate review the outstanding student loans and create a schedule for monthly payment amounts. Then help draw up a budget that will make sure those amounts can be paid.

LOOK AT ALTERNATIVES
If the budget doesn't balance, your child needs to either increase income or decrease expenses. Try to gently suggest ways that this can be accomplished. If the monthly payments are too high in relation to monthly income, take a look at loan consolidation or income-based repayment options, especially with the federal student loans. Your student might think that you will be disappointed because

this could be perceived as a failure, but provide assurance that you are proud of what has been accomplished so far. A willingness to acknowledge problems, seek assistance, and search for possible solutions is a tremendous skill to have in place early in adult life.

HELP WITH COMMUNICATION

It may be necessary to actually talk to some of the lenders in question. Help your child gather the necessary information, put together discussion points regarding the current financial situation, and list questions that need to be addressed. For example:

- What is the total amount currently due?
- What are my options for getting up to date with payments?
- Do you offer consolidation, forbearance, or deferral options?
- What are the requirements for any programs that you have for borrowers who are behind on payments?

You can sit there while your child makes the call and listen on speaker, but try not to interrupt or take over the conversation. This is a good learning experience that will provide your child with some necessary communication skills.

It is hard to see your child going through difficult times. You may be tempted to try to solve the problem or just pay off the student loans yourself, but is this really the best solution to the problem? Nothing will be learned using this approach. If you have the funds available, you could offer to pay them as a loan, but you must make it clear that your child will be responsible for making payments to you. Write down the terms, and have your student sign the note. Your role otherwise is to serve as guidance counselor, confidant, financial adviser, and moral supporter to help your now-adult learn to take on challenges and come up with solutions.

LOOK AT WAYS TO INCREASE INCOME

There are two parts to a budget: income and expenses. If your student's budget is not in balance, they either have to increase income or decrease expenses. You can help them look around to determine if there are any ways to increase their income. Perhaps it's time to look for a higher-paying job now that the economy is improving, or you may have to look for part-time work at night or on the weekends.

It may be possible to earn extra money through freelance consulting, tutoring, writing, web design, or editing. If they are artistic or crafty, selling their creations online may be an option. People who are handy at fixing things or good at spotting a bargain might be able to set up an eBay or Amazon business to find items to buy at one price, fix them up, and sell them at a higher price. Those who are good at social media can offer consulting services to local businesses and manage their online presence for a specified amount each week. Who knows, they might even find that they become good enough at their part-time gig to turn it into a full-time career!

REDUCE EXPENSES

This is something nobody really likes to think about, but it can make a big difference in a personal budget. Ask your graduate to think about some important questions:

- Do you need to move into an apartment by yourself right away, or can you find a roommate or stay with your parents for a year?
- Do you need a brand-new car right after graduation, or can you survive with a solid used car for a few years while you are making student loan payments?
- How many times per week do you need to go out, and are there times when you can find something that is free or inexpensive to do?
- Do you need the best cell phone, texting, and data plan, or can you survive with a lower level of service?
- When you look at your budget line items, where can you cut back?

When they take some time to look at where the money is going, they might be surprised at how much spending is completely unnecessary. As a society, we spend an awful lot of money on things that are nice to have, but not really basic necessities. When your graduate looks at what can be cut out of the budget for a year, with those savings redirected to student loan payments, it's remarkable what can be achieved. Plus, thrifty skills will serve you well at any financial level.

PAYMENT HELP

As we discussed in Chapter 8, the federal government and private lenders typically have a few options for borrowers who either can't afford their payments or who fall behind on them. They include:

- **Deferment:** This option allows you to temporarily put your principal and interest payments on hold. During this time, the government may pay the interest on Direct Subsidized Loans. The borrower is responsible for paying interest that accumulates on PLUS loans and unsubsidized loans during the deferment period, but payment is not due until the deferment period ends.

- **Forbearance:** With this option, you may be allowed to stop making payments or reduce your monthly payment for up to 12 months. Interest continues to accrue on both your subsidized and unsubsidized loans. Borrowers may be eligible for forbearance due to financial hardship, illness, medical residency, certain teaching programs, or military service. Be careful here: You will end up paying more in the end. The payments you don't make are added on to the loan's principal balance, and interest accrues on them until the loan is paid off. Make sure your child reads all terms carefully and understands the financial consequences before they opt for forbearance.

- **Loan consolidation:** With consolidation, you wrap all your student loans into one. This can be a big convenience because you only make one payment each month. However, depending on whether you choose a Direct Consolidation Loan, if that's an option, or consolidation through a private lender, terms may differ. Since repayment terms may be longer, you might end up repaying more money in the long run. Benefits associated with the original loan, such as interest rate discounts, principal rebates, or other loan features may be lost, so be sure your child checks the fine print before they choose this option.

Staying on the Right Track

Perhaps your student isn't struggling with student loans or has gotten caught up. Encourage them to consider making additional principal payments—even if it's before the six-month grace period ends. Even $100 extra per month can make a big difference over the life of the loan. Visit my website, CollegeFinancialAidAdvisors.com, to find tools like a calculator you can use to see the impact additional principal payments can have.

Once your student has these financial skills lodged in their brain, they're there for other financial choices in life. Knowing how to use debt wisely can help them handle credit cards better and provide them with the background needed to evaluate options when it comes time to borrow money again for anything from a new car to a new home. Debt is not a bad thing. When taken on with proper thought and consideration, it can help achieve a goal, such as obtaining a college education. The problem is when people borrow more than they need, spend the proceeds unwisely, and don't think about how they are going to repay the loan when it comes due in the future.

THE BOTTOM LINE

- Teach your student about the importance of student loans and staying ahead of them. Falling behind or defaulting can have very serious consequences.
- Work with your child to find solutions to student loan problems, but don't take over payments unless that was the original plan. Working with your child to find solutions will impart better financial skills.
- Contact the lender and explore deferment, forbearance, and consolidation options, but know what you're getting into.
- Encourage your son or daughter to make additional principal payments to pay off the loan faster and decrease the amount of interest paid over time.

12

Congratulations, You Made It!

PLANNING FOR AND SEEING YOUR CHILD through obtaining a post-secondary education is an enormous feat. Just as your son or daughter should be proud of themselves for completing a degree, you should be proud for seeing them through it. Your "baby" has transitioned into an adult. It's important to celebrate the occasion.

In the best case, your relationship with your son or daughter has evolved, too. You've been through a challenging experience together where you had to plan, work hard, and trust in each other. By openly communicating about money and financial goals and challenges, the tenor of your relationship may have changed. Your child has the skills to go out into the world and be a financially responsible citizen.

WHAT NOW?

You may have other children who are in or going to college, so the process may repeat itself. This book is structured so you can return to it for insight and help at any point in the financial aid process. In addition, I regularly add new content to my website, www.CollegeFinancialAidAdvisors. com. Since various thresholds, practices, and deadlines change from year to year, be sure to sign up for our newsletter, where we'll announce such changes and additions on our website. That way, you'll always have the most up-to-date information.

Once you've gotten all your children through school, it's time to focus on you again. It's probably been a long time since you've had the freedom to do so. However, as a parent who went through the process twice, I can tell you there is great joy in watching your children find themselves and eventually soar. It's OK if it doesn't happen immediately. But by being there for them and being open and honest, your children always have a place to call "home."

I wish you all the best as you navigate this process and invite you to contact me through my website with questions or success stories. There, I also have several webinars and a blog with the latest financial aid information. You can also find me on Twitter, @JodiOkun, where I tweet all sorts of news about college and financial aid.

Glossary

ACT: A standardized test given to high school students that assesses academic readiness for college. The test consists of subject area tests in English, math, reading, and science, along with a writing test.

Attending School: The college, university, or other school at which the student matriculates.

Award Amount: The amount of aid the student will receive from their attending school based on their current grant and loan eligibility, enrollment, Expected Family Contribution (EFC), and the school's cost of attendance (COA).

Award Letter: An offer from a college or professional/career school that states the amount of financial aid the family is eligible for upon acceptance and registration.

Award Year: School year and/or academic term for which financial aid is used to fund a student's education. The award year begins on July 1 and ends on June 30 of the following year.

Bursar: The college official responsible for handling all needs, including payments, pertaining to tuition billing, housing, fees, and other related expenses.

College Scholarship Service (CSS) Profile: A financial aid application required by some schools that is distributed by the College Board. The CSS Profile takes a closer look at the financial background of a student and their family. The CSS Profile is more detailed than the FAFSA and determines a student's financial aid using institutional methodology.

Consolidation: The process of combining all loans into a new, single loan.

Cost of Attendance (COA): The total cost amount required to attend a particular school. COA includes tuition and fees, room and board, allowances for books, supplies, loan fees, transportation, and other miscellaneous and personal expenses.

Dependent Student: A student who does not meet any of the independent student criteria.

Direct Consolidation Loan: A federal loan made by the U.S. Department of Education that allows a student to combine multiple federal student loans into one new loan.

Direct Loan: A federal loan that eligible students and parents borrow directly from the U.S. Department of Education. Federal loans include Direct Subsidized Loans, Direct Unsubsidized Loans, and Direct PLUS Loans.

Disbursement: Funds paid out from resources, such as student loans, grants, scholarships, etc.

Endorser: A co-signer on a loan who does not have an adverse credit history and who agrees to repay the loan if the borrower does not repay.

Enrollment Status: Reported by the student's attending school, indicating whether the student is (or was) full time, part time, withdrawn, etc.

Expected Family Contribution (EFC): The number colleges use to determine eligibility for federal financial aid. The EFC is calculated from information that is provided in the FAFSA.

Federal Pell Grant: A program that awards money to eligible undergraduate students in financial need that does not need to be repaid.

Federal Student Aid (FSA): Financial aid from the federal government to help pay for college tuition and expenses.

Financial Aid Offer: The total amount of federal and nonfederal aid offered to a student by their attending school.

Financial Aid Office: The office at the student's school that is responsible for preparing and communicating information about all financial aid.

Free Application for Federal Student Aid (FAFSA): A form completed annually by current and prospective college students to determine their eligibility for financial aid.

FSA ID: The username and password combination for students and parents used as an identifier to access individual financial aid information.

Grant: Financial aid that does not need to be repaid.

Independent Student: A student that meets any of these qualifications: at least 24 years old, married, a graduate or professional student, a veteran, a member of the armed forces, an orphan, a ward of the court, someone with legal dependents other than a spouse, an emancipated minor, or someone who is homeless or at risk of becoming homeless.

Interest: A periodic fee for borrowing money from a private or federal lender that is expressed as a percentage of the balance of the loan.

Lender: The organization that provides the initial loan.

Lifetime Eligibility Used (LEU): The amount of all Federal Pell Grant aid (in percentage) awarded to a student, divided by the amount of Pell Grant aid you would have been eligible to receive based on full-time enrollment. The amount of Federal Pell Grants awarded to a student is limited by federal law to be the equivalent of six years of Pell Grant funding.

Loan Date: The date on which the borrower receives the first disbursement of their loan.

Master Promissory Note (MPN): A binding legal document that you must sign when you get a federal student loan that lists the terms and conditions under which you agree to repay the loan and explains your rights and responsibilities as a borrower.

Merit-based Aid: Aid provided based on skills or ability (e.g., academic merit for high grades).

Need-based Aid: Aid provided based on financial need.

Net Price: The difference between the full cost to attend college or a career school minus any grants or scholarships for which the student is eligible.

Net Price Calculator: A free tool provided to students that allows them to calculate their net price for any university or college of interest.

PLUS Loan: A federal loan that graduate or professional-degree students and parents of dependent undergraduate students can obtain to help pay education expenses.

Principal: The total sum of money that the borrower owes, including the interest that capitalizes.

Priority Date: The date on which your application—whether it's for financial aid, college admissions, housing, etc.—should be received in order to get the strongest consideration.

Private Loan: A nonfederal loan provided by a lender to a borrower. Private loans can come from banks, credit unions, or schools.

Room and Board: The housing and food expenses associated with tuition costs.

SAT: A standardized test widely used for college admission in the U.S. The test measures math and reading literacy and writing skills needed for collegiate academic success.

Scholarship: Money awarded to students based on academic, athletic, or other criteria used for education expenses.

State Aid: Aid provided by a student's state of legal residency.

Status Effective Date: The date that a current loan becomes effective.

Student Aid Report (SAR): A summary of the information provided on the FAFSA application.

Subsidized Loan: A loan based on financial need for which interest does not accrue or on which the federal government pays the interest that accrues when the borrower is in school, during the loan's six-month grace period, or when it is in deferred payment status.[7]

Tuition: The total sum of money it costs for classes at an educational institution.

Unsubsidized Loan: A loan provided to a borrower in which they are fully responsible for paying the interest regardless of the loan status. Interest on unsubsidized loans accrues from the date of disbursement and continues throughout the life of the loan.

Verification: The process in which colleges verify the data provided on the FAFSA. Colleges may request documentation to prove information reported by a family.

Work-Study Program: A federal student aid program that provides part-time jobs to students enrolled in school, which helps to pay for academic expenses.

End Notes

1. National Center for Education Statistics website, "Annual Earnings of Young Adults," May 2015. http://nces.ed.gov/programs/coe/indicator_cba.asp

2. Bankrate.com, "Pros and cons of prepaid college tuition plans," by Christina Couch. http://www.bankrate.com/finance/college-finance/pros-and-cons-of-prepaid-tuition-plans-1.aspx

3. The ACT website, Frequently Asked Questions. http://www.act.org/content/act/en/products-and-services/the-act/help.html

4. College Board website, "Retaking the SAT." https://collegereadiness.collegeboard.org/sat/scores/understanding-scores

5. National Center for Education Statistics website, Fast Facts, "Time to Degree," 2011. https://nces.ed.gov/fastfacts/display.asp?id=569

6. TaxFormCalculator.com. http://www.taxformcalculator.com/tax/40000.html

7. Federal Student Aid website, https://studentaid.ed.gov/sa/glossary#Independent_Student

Index

A

achievements, student, 30, 78, 109

ACT (achievement test), 39-40, 52-55, 56

admission decisions, 45-48

admissions tests, 33, 39-40, 52-55, 56

allowances, 62-63

applying for college. *See* college applications

applying for financial aid. *See* CSS Profile; Free Application for Federal Student Aid

assessments for college readiness, 33, 39-40, 52-55, 56

athletic scholarships, 114-115. *See also* scholarships

award amounts, 35, 104, 106, 118-119. *See also* financial aid; financial aid planning

award letters, 77, 104, 116-117, 123

award process, 3-5, 76-77

B

bankruptcy, 150. *See also* financial skills training; money management

BigFuture by College Board, 112

borrowing strategies, 9-10, 123, 127-133, 135. *See also* student loans

budgeting, 62, 65-68, 129, 145, 156-157, 163, 171-172. *See also* financial skills training; money management

C

campus visits, 36-38

career and college interests, 24-25, 30-32, 35-36

CareerOneStop.com, 112

Chegg.com, 113

COA (cost of attendance), 19, 35, 76, 117-118, 128. *See also* net price

college applications. *See also* financial aid

    admission decisions and, 45-48

    admissions tests and, 33, 39-40, 52-55, 56

    Common Application, 49

    deadlines for, 45-48, 49-50

    essay requirements in, 49-52

    filling out, 50-52

    following up after submitting, 56

    grades and, 34, 38, 46, 56, 100

    interviews and, 56

    preparation list for completing, 51

    scheduling tasks for completing, 50

    school requirements for, 49

    social media and, 55-56

    starting the process, 44-48

    tasks after submitting, 56-57

    timeline for, 57-59

College Board's Net Price Calculator, 106

college freshmen, 141-152. *See also* financial skills training; money management

college graduates, 10-11, 117-118, 158-163, 164, 167-175. *See also* student loans

college interviews, 56

college lists, 30-31, 32, 35-36, 41

College Scholarship Service (CSS) Profile, 34, 79-81, 83, 88, 98, 104. *See also* financial aid; financial aid planning; Free Application for Federal Student Aid

college seniors, 153-163. *See also* college graduates; financial skills training; student loans

Common Application, 49

community involvement, 23, 29-30

consolidating student loans, 126-127, 134-136, 173-174. *See also* student loans

corporate scholarships, 113. *See also* scholarships

cost of attendance (COA), 19, 35, 76, 117-118, 128. *See also* net price

cost of attending college, 65-68

credit cards, 69-70, 131, 144, 148, 174

credit check, 126

credit reports, 149

CSS Profile, 34, 79-81, 83, 88, 98, 104. *See also* financial aid; financial aid planning; Free Application for Federal Student Aid

D

debt, 123, 144-145, 155-156, 159-163, 174-175. *See also* financial skills training; money management

debt repayment calculators, 156

defaulting on loans, 122, 136, 147-148, 151, 167. *See also* repaying student loans; student loans

deferring loan repayment, 126, 136-137, 163, 173. *See also* repaying student loans; student loans

Direct Consolidation Loans, 126

Direct PLUS Loans, 123-125, 173

Direct Subsidized Loans, 123-124, 126, 173
Direct Unsubsidized Loans, 107-108, 123-124, 173
Discover Student Loans, 113, 127, 132

E
early action admission, 45-46
early decision admission, 46-47, 48
EFC (Expected Family Contribution), 76, 95, 98
elementary school scholarships, 21. *See also* scholarships
employment post-graduation, 117-118
essay requirements in applications, 49-52
estimating tools, 106
Expected Family Contribution (EFC), 76, 95, 98
extracurricular activities, 29-30

F
FAFSA. *See* Free Application for Federal Student Aid
FAFSA4caster, 104, 106
federal aid, 100-101, 105-109, 123-125, 126. *See also* financial aid;
financial aid planning
Federal Student Aid (FSA) ID, 93-94
Federal Supplemental Educational Opportunity Grants (FSEOG), 107.
See also federal aid
Federal Work-Study (FWS) Program, 77, 80, 108-109. *See also*
federal aid; financial aid
financial aid
      applying for. *See* CSS Profile; Free Application for Federal
Student Aid
      award amounts, 35, 104, 106, 118-119
      award letters, 77, 104, 116-117, 123

estimating tools, 106

factors affecting eligibility for, 104

federal aid, 100-101, 105-109, 123-125, 126

free money, 9-10, 104, 128

grades and, 34, 38, 56, 100

maximizing, 97-98

myths and assumptions about, 16-17, 98-102

negotiating aid packages, 118-119

order of, 9-10

prepaid tuition programs and, 24-25

qualifying for, 79-85

review and award process, 3-5, 76-77

types of, 77-79, 99-100, 104-105

financial aid planning. *See also* money management

advantages of starting early, 17, 75

career and college interests and, 24-25, 30-32, 35-36

considerations in, 17-18

financial need calculation in, 76

529 savings plans, 21, 24-25, 81-82

free money in, 9-10, 104, 128

in high school freshman year, 29-31

in high school junior year, 33-41

in high school senior year, 34

in high school sophomore year, 31-33

involving students in, 8

in middle school years, 17-25

money-saving strategies, 18-20, 24-25, 40

prepaid tuition programs, 24-25

reviewing your plan, 18

starting, 5, 7-8, 17, 22-23, 43-44

financial need, calculating, 76

financial skills training. *See also* money management

    benefit of, 177-178

    college freshmen, 141-152

    college graduates, 164, 167-175

    college seniors, 153-163

    graduate students, 163-165

    high school students, 31, 32-35, 40, 62-71, 127-130

    setting savings goals, 32-33

529 savings plans, 21, 24-25, 81-82. *See also* financial aid planning

fixed interest rates, 125-126

forbearance, 136-137, 173. *See also* repaying student loans; student loans

forgiveness, cancellation, and discharge of loans, 137. *See also* student loans

Free Application for Federal Student Aid (FAFSA). *See also* CSS Profile; financial aid; financial aid planning

    completing the form, 79-81, 92-95, 104

    correcting information after submission of, 96-97

    deadlines for submission, 89-90, 94

    documentation checklist for, 93

    financial information to be included in, 79-85, 90-92

    how colleges use information from, 88-89

    maximizing amount of aid and, 97-98

    myths about, 98-102

    processing time, 94-95

    reviewing Student Aid Reports for errors, 95-96

    verification process, 96-97

    when to file, 34

    who should complete it, 90

free money, 9-10, 104, 128. *See also* financial aid; financial aid planning

freshman year in college, 141-152. *See also* financial skills training; money management

freshman year in high school, 28-31. *See also* financial aid planning; financial skills training

FSA ID, 93-94

FSEOG (Federal Supplemental Educational Opportunity Grants), 107. *See also* federal aid

FWS (Federal Work-Study) Program, 77, 80, 108-109. *See also* federal aid; financial aid

G

grades, 22, 34, 38, 46, 56, 100

graduate school students, 163-165

graduating college seniors, 158-163, 164. *See also* college graduates; student loans

graduation rates, 117-118

grants, 105-108. *See also* federal aid; financial aid; financial aid planning

H

high school freshman year, 28-31. *See also* financial aid planning; financial skills training

high school junior year, 33-41. *See also* college applications; financial skills training

high school senior year, 34, 44-45, 49-50, 55-57. *See also* college applications; Free Application for Federal Student Aid

high school sophomore year, 31-33. *See also* financial aid planning; financial skills training

home improvements, 83

I

inheritances, 83-84

interest on loans, 100, 107-108, 124-126, 133, 135, 136, 163, 173. *See also* student loans

interviews, college, 56

Iraq and Afghanistan Service Grants, 108. *See also* federal aid

J

junior year in high school, 33-41. *See also* college applications; financial skills training

L

late-deadline scholarships, 113-114, 119. *See also* scholarships

leadership roles, 23

life skills, 11, 23-24, 174-175

living expenses, 157-159

loan consolidation, 126-127, 134-136, 173-174. *See also* repaying student loans

loan forgiveness, cancellation, and discharge, 137. *See also* repaying student loans

loans. *See* student loans

M

merit-based financial aid, 77, 78-79. *See also* financial aid; financial aid planning

middle school years, 17-25. *See also* financial aid planning

millennial generation, 70-71

money management. *See also* financial aid planning; financial skills training

      borrowing, 9-10, 123, 127-133, 135

budgeting, 62, 65-68, 129, 145, 156-157, 163, 171-172
  controlling costs and spending, 128-129
  good practices in, 150-152, 174-175
  living expenses, 157-159
  living on the edge and, 149
  poor money management, 147-151
  savings goals for students, 32-33
money-saving strategies, 18-20, 24-25, 40. *See also* 529 savings plans
mortgages, 83
moving costs, 160
myths and assumptions about financial aid, 16-17, 98-102

N
need-based financial aid, 77-78, 80. *See also* financial aid; financial aid planning
negotiating aid packages, 118-119. *See also* financial aid; financial aid planning
net price, 106. *See also* cost of attendance
Net Price Calculator, 106
non-need-based financial aid, 78, 80. *See also* financial aid; financial aid planning

P
part-time work, 9-10, 25, 31, 32-33, 128. *See also* Federal Work-Study Program
Pell Grants, 106. *See also* federal aid
personal statements, 49. *See also* essay requirements in applications
PLUS Loans, 123-125

poor money management, 147-151. *See also* financial skills training; money management

post-graduation employment record, 117-118

Preliminary SAT/National Merit Scholarship Qualifying Test (PSAT/NMSQT), 33. *See also* SAT

prepaid tuition programs, 24-25. *See also* financial aid planning

preparation resources for admissions tests, 53-54. *See also* admissions tests

private middle schools, 20-21. *See also* middle school years

private student loans, 125-127. *See also* student loans

PSAT/NMSQT (Preliminary SAT/National Merit Scholarship Qualifying Test), 33. *See also* SAT

R

references, 30

regular admission, 47-48

repaying student loans, 122-123, 126-127, 133-137, 167-175. *See also* defaulting on loans; student loans

repayment calculators, 156

resumes, 38-39

retirement accounts, 82-83

rolling admission, 48

S

SAT (aptitude test), 33, 39-40, 52-55

savings goals, 32-33

scholarships. *See also* financial aid; financial aid planning

    applying for, 115-116

    basic information about, 109-110

    elementary and middle school, 21

maximizing, 128

sources for finding, 109-115, 119

types of, 21, 109-110, 113-115

Scholarships.com, 112

senior year in high school, 34, 44-45, 49-50, 55-57. *See also* college applications; financial skills training; Free Application for Federal Student Aid

senioritis, 56

single choice early action admission, 46

situational financial aid, 79. *See also* financial aid; financial aid planning

social media, 55-56

sophomore year in high school, 31-33. *See also* financial aid planning; financial skills training

Student Aid Report, 95-96

student loan bubble, 123

student loans. *See also* financial aid; financial aid planning

    considering, 8-9, 119-120, 127-133

    consolidating, 126-127, 134-136, 173-174

    defaulting on, 122, 136, 147-148, 151, 167

    deferring repayment, 126, 136-137, 163, 173

    determining how much to borrow, 135

    discussing repayment with lenders, 170-171

    discussing with students, 8-9

    federal, 123-125, 126

    fees for, 124-125, 127

    forbearance of, 136-137, 173

    forgiveness, cancellation and discharge, 137

    interest on, 100, 107-108, 124-126, 133, 135, 136, 163, 173

    overborrowing, 123

private, 125-127
repaying, 122-123, 126-127, 133-137, 167-175
repayment help, 173-175
repercussions for not repaying, 122
types of, 123-127
study habits, 23, 29
subsidized loans, 123-124, 126, 173. *See also* student loans
summer before high school senior year, 44-45. *See also* college applications; financial aid planning

T
Teacher Education Assistance for College and Higher Education (TEACH) Grants, 107-108. *See also* federal aid

U
unsubsidized loans, 107-108, 123-124, 173. *See also* student loans
U.S. Department of Education, 112

V
variable interest rates, 126

W
work-study programs, 9, 77, 104. *See also* federal aid; financial aid

CPSIA information can be obtained
at www.ICGtesting.com
Printed in the USA
LVOW04*2020070716
495480LV00017B/145/P